JULES CHOPPIN
(1830–1914)

New Orleans Poems
in Creole and French

English Versions by

NORMAN R. SHAPIRO

Introduction by

M. LYNN WEISS

Jules Choppin

New Orleans Poems in Creole and French

Second Line Press wishes to thank Wesleyan University for its support.
Publication of this book has been aided by a grant from the Thomas and
Catharine McMahon Fund of Wesleyan University, established through the
generosity of the late Joseph McMahon.

Second Line Press and Black Widow Press are imprints of Common-
wealth Books, Inc. Please direct all queries to Commonwealth Books, 9
Spring Lane, Boston, MA 02109 USA.

Distributed to the trade by NBN (National Book Network) through-
out North America, Canada, and the U.K., all books from Second Line
Press and Black Widow Press are printed on acid-free paper and glued into
bindings. Second Line Press and Black Widow Press and their logos are
registered trademarks of Commonwealth Books, Inc.

Joseph S. Phillips and Susan J. Wood, Ph.D., Publishers
www.blackwidowpress.com

Book production and design: Kerrie Kemperman

Cover image: House for Napoleon. St. Louis and Chartres Streets. Wm.
Woodward / ca. 1900. Image © The Historic New Orleans Collection. Gift
of Laura Simon Nelson. Acc. No. 2006.0430.18

ISBN-13: 978-0-9889627-7-4

Printed in the United States

10 9 8 7 6 5 4 3 2 1

for Wernor Sollors,
teacher, colleague, friend

TABLE OF CONTENTS

POEMS IN FRENCH

PREFACE

Long interested in francophone Louisiana literature, I first became acquainted with the engaging poetry of Jules Choppin while combing through the Comptes-rendus de l'Athénée Louisianais in search of poets to translate and include in *Creole Echoes: The Francophone Poetry of Nineteenth-Century Louisiana*. A few years later, I contributed several of the resulting translations, of Choppin and others, to a special number of *Metamorphoses*.

The Choppin poems caught the attention of the poet's great-grandson Gil Choppin, of Houston, who asked if I had more to share with him and his family. At the time, I didn't. But, thanks to his enthusiasm, the idea occurred to me, indeed, to expand the collection.

The result is the present volume, which, modest though it is, represents almost the totality of Choppin's works, in both standard French and Louisiana Creole. I thank Gil Choppin not only for inspiring it, but also for attending it along the way, and generously providing it with many useful details, otherwise lost.

My very special thanks as well to my frequent collaborator M. Lynn Weiss for expertly placing Jules Choppin in his francophone, and yet very American, historico-literary context, and to Joseph Phillips of Black Widow Press for his confidence in adding the work to his others of Louisiana inspiration.

INTRODUCTION

This collection, *Jules Choppin (1830–1914): New Orleans Poems in Creole and French,* contributes to the ongoing effort to recover forgotten treasures from 19th-century francophone American literature. The Tintamarre project at Centenary College, has created an impressive archive of nineteenth-century texts in the original French, available online and in print [i]. Still, very few of these texts have been translated into English. Those works that are available in English include Victor Séjour's short story, "The Mulatto," and three of his plays: *The Brown Overcoat, The Jew of Seville (Diégarias),* and *The Fortune Teller* [ii]. There is a selection of poetry by Creoles, Creoles of color, and freed bondsmen in Norman Shapiro's and my bilingual anthology, *Creole Echoes: The Francophone Poetry of Nineteenth-Century Louisiana,* including two poems by Jules Choppin [iii]. Most recently, a translation of excerpts from Charles Testut's monumental abolitionist novel, *Le Vieux Solomon, ou une Famille d'Esclaves au xix Siècle. (Old Solomon; or, a Slave Family in the Nineteenth Century)* appeared in 2010 [iv]. The anthologies and individual works by Louisiana's francophone writers offer students, scholars, and the casual reader, an in-depth and detailed picture of the cultural and historical milieu in which these writers worked. More importantly, Louisiana's francophone literature deepens the knowledge and appreciation of our American literary tradition and makes meaningful our multicultural origins [v]. More, it reminds us of how those origins complicate, as they create, what it meant and means to be an "American." Jules Choppin's contribution to this archive is especially important because he wrote some of the best poetry in Louisiana Creole.

That patois was the local dialect of Louisiana that grew out of two centuries of daily contact between speakers of French and Spanish, and those who spoke African and Native American languages and whose lives and labors intersected in every possible way. Creole was Louisiana's lingua franca. Choppin had an ear for (and appreciation of) this patois. Although some would balk at the suggestion of translating La Fontaine into the dialect of a far-flung colony, Choppin's renditions made the familiar fables local, fresh, and funny. Nor was he the only "colonial" to do so. And when the narrator is a slave or former slave, the "moral," is all the more salient.

Unlike his parents and siblings, Jules Choppin was born in Louisiana in 1830, making him the first Creole in his immediate family [vi]. He grew up on a sugar plantation in St. James Parish, "Home Place," owned by his first cousin Louis Valérien Choppin. There he received his primary education and, in 1850, he left the plantation to further his education at Georgetown College (later Georgetown University). When he returned to St. James Parish, he became the tutor for the Fortier children, an elite Creole family. At the end of the Civil War, Choppin joined the faculty at Tulane University, as a professor of French language and literature. At Tulane, Choppin encountered one of his former students, Alcée Fortier, now a professor of Louisiana History. This would be a fortuitous reunion for both men [vii].

It is difficult to overstate Fortier's role in the presentation, promotion, and preservation of Louisiana's francophone literature. The first President of the Modern Language Association, Alcée Fortier recognized and embraced the bilingual, bicultural reality of Louisiana in his own day and at the dawn of the twentieth-century. He spoke and wrote with native fluency in both languages. In his famous 1886 essay, "French Literature in Louisiana," Fortier introduced Anglo-Americans to the literature of their francophone kinsmen [viii]. This essay determined the study of Louisiana history and literature for the next fifty years. In 1876, Fortier, Alfred Mercier, and other members of the Creole class, founded l'Athénée Louisianais, a literary society intended to support and encourage the continued use of French in Louisiana. Almost all of Jules Choppin's poetry was published in *Comptes-rendus*, the organ of l'Athénée Louisianais [ix]. We are deeply indebted to the foresight of its founders:

were it not for *Comptes-rendus*, most of the post-bellum literature of Louisiana would have been lost or never written. Unlike publishing practices in the North, almost all of Louisiana's poetry was published in newspapers or journals, in French or in bilingual editions which, after the War, became almost extinct. *Comptes-rendus* was created to fill that vacuum.

A brief history of publishing in Louisiana underscores the significance of *Comptes-rendus*. Louisiana's first newspaper, *Le Moniteur de la Louisiane* appeared in 1794 and remained the only such paper until 1803. Louisiana's change in status from U.S. territory (1803) to state (1812) prompted the establishment of several more newspapers. In 1830 (fortuitously the year of Choppin's birth), newspapers began to print poetry, but then only occasionally. Ultimately, the publication of literature in newspapers and journals, in the ante-bellum period, flourished. The first small weekly or monthly arts journals appeared in the early 1840s, of which *Revue Louisianaise* (1846–1848) was among the best [x]. This golden age (1830–1860) included bilingual publications and editions in other European languages and illustrated the emergence of New Orleans as a major multicultural city. At the same time, French as the lingua franca of Louisiana was undermined by several factors, the most important of which was immigration.

Between 1810 and 1830, approximately 10,000 refugees from the Haitian Revolution of 1804 found their way to New Orleans, swelling the French-speaking Creoles and Creoles of color population from 4,000 to 16,710 [xi]. And although Anglophone immigrants had trickled down the Mississippi to New Orleans since 1803, in the 1840s large waves of German immigrants arrived, contributing to the American Babel. Residents of ante-bellum New Orleans took for granted the availability of newspapers in French and English or bilingual editions; there was even a New Orleans paper published briefly in German, *Louisiana Staats-Zeitung* (1854–1855) [xii]. In addition to the influx of non-French speakers, Louisiana's status as a francophone state in an English-only nation, was anathema.

By 1896 only six French-language newspapers and journals were still in circulation. In 1914 the death knell sounded for French in Louisiana when the government no longer required that its documents be published in English and French [xiii]. With the disappearance of francophone newspapers, *Comptes-rendus* became more than a literary journal; it was the repository and archive of a bygone era, evidence of a unique time and place.

In the 1894 volume *Louisiana Studies*, Alcée Fortier asserted, "Our contemporary literature is contained almost exclusively in *Comptes-rendus de l'Athénée Louisianais...*" [xiv]. Before his death in 1914, between 1896 and 1905, Jules Choppin had contributed approximately thirty-six poems to *Comptes-rendus* [xv–xvi]. Choppin's poetry resembles that of his predecessors in its celebration of Louisiana's natural settings, specifically the bayou. As in traditional Romantic poetry, Nature assumes a God-like role; its power redeems the soul and restores the body, and sanctifies the European presence in the "new" world. For example, Dr. Alfred Mercier's "Fatherland" celebrates a homecoming: "O Meschacébé! You saw me rejoice / In childish games by your resounding shore; / Father of Waters, you see me once more / Leap, drunk with joy, to hear your long-drawn voice!" [xvii]. The Mississippi is Mercier's "Fatherland." The Mississippi and the bayou unambiguously define the natural settings of the American South, and specifically Louisiana. Among the six poems with "bayou" in their title or first line, Choppin's "My Old Bayou Saint-Jean" begins, "How beautiful, the bayou mine! I love / Its twists and turns, the air wafting above... / It snakes in silence through the reeds, amid / Reflected giants..." Like Mercier's Mississippi, in "My Old Bayou Saint-Jean," Choppin's bayou comforts, encourages reflection, and inspires the imagination. Interestingly, these poems often begin with an invocation of the bayou, but can then become a love-song to the bayou, a paean to the stars, or a vehement curse on man's depravity. However God-like, in every poem, the bayou is an old friend, who listens with understanding and compassion.

Each of the Creole narratives ascribed to "Pa Guitin," an "old black man from St-Jacquois," demands an oral reading. In "Chat on the Twelve Months of the Year," "Pa Guitin's" young audience discovers the life of a slave through vivid descriptions of the months of each season. Ice-cold January means cutting cane, sunup to sundown, with little more to eat than molasses and grits: "Eat, young folk, then go sleep. Come dawn, no stay / In bed... Up! Up!... Like on nice summer day. / But you sleep late, too long, lie flat on back, / And oh! You wrong! Pay price: Whip crack, go clak!" The September poem juxtaposes and intersperses the speaker of Creole with that of standard French:

> "Time for make hay. Time for chop wood, go fetch..."
> —That vile patois! What can he mean, black wretch?
> "Him there... Make fun... Him treat me like no-good!"
> —I thought I heard him mention time, hay, wood...
> "Him watch tongue, or me knock on ass! Him see!"
> —What rage rings in his voice! Is it for me?

The contrast is humorous because it makes the most of the differences between Creole and standard French. Even though the patois is rife with errors, the speaker's French is formal to a fault and he is ridiculed for being obtuse and figuratively deaf.

Life of a black man or woman (often a slave) is recounted (in Creole) in the animal trickster tales, adaptations of La Fontaine and others. "The Wolf and the Dog" is especially instructive. Butch, a well-fed farm dog, tries to convince the hungry wolf to change places with him. M'sieu Wolf is almost "sold" on the idea until he sees a scar on Butch's neck. When M'sieu Wolf learns that he would have to be chained, he runs for his life and exclaims: "Back to wood! Freedom, night and day, / Beat café crème and fine pâté!..." The Monkey and the Leopard" is an adaptation of a fable by Florian [xviii]. A group of monkeys at play make so much noise banging, clanging, laughing, singing, and clapping that they disturb the Leopard's sleep. Seeing him, the monkeys become alarmed. Sweetly he assures them that he simply wants to play. But when he is close enough he takes a strong, swift, swipe, and "…blood flow free…" The conclusion: "So listen, you no play game with 'big buck!' / Paw turn to claw, and you get big bad luck! / Watch out! Them give you sugar word, but might / Come open jaw up wide and take good bite!" From which, the moral: "Best monkey stay with friend what know them!" One can easily see in this adaptation an allusion to the relationship between slave and master.

In "The Monkeys and the Leopard" and "The Tortoise and the Hare" Norman Shapiro's brilliant rendering of sound and movement imbue these fables with fresh animation. The playful monkeys awaken the Leopard when they "…laugh and play / Together, clap hand, bash and bang and slap… / Play, shout, have fine old time. Jump all around…" The vitality of these lines is created with monosyllabic action-verbs and is amplified by repetitious syntax; the eardrum-stabbing percussion of the monkeys' banging, clapping, clanging cacophony is almost too loud to imagine. [1] Creole transforms "The Hare and the Tortoise" from a familiar fable into an animated, vivid, and hilarious story. In this version, Madame Turtle and Rabbit are friends. So, when Madame Turtle suggests the race, Rabbit laughs: "You crazy so-and-so! / Lazy old stick-in-mud! Me Rabbit! Bah!" Knowing Rabbit's vanity, the clever Turtle replies: "You scared you lose! You only good for play, / And for go nibble cabbage every day!" Confident of his victory, Rabbit wastes time. His dawdling is amusing because it is so intentional. Even napping he embodies the movement that the verbs create: "… him dart / Back, forth… Lie down, take nap… Get up, no hurry… / Jump, dance, do jig…" The action is vivid, lively, and funny. (Rabbit resembles Bugs Bunny in action and attitude). Madame Turtle's "Plok, plok plok plok…" preceding Rabbit's "whish" ends the tale. The onomatopoeia, "plok, plok plok plok" and "whish," makes it difficult to accept Rabbit's defeat. Replicating sound, whether it is "whish" or "clak" or words and syntax put into Creole, is what makes Choppin's renditions of the familiar fresh despite the passage of time and the many renditions of the Aesopic original.

The language or dialect of the marginalized, immigrants, indentured servants, or slaves has always had an impact on the standard language. It revitalizes the standard language by disrupting the habitual ways in which we use it. This is especially evident in the United States where some claim, disparagingly, that English has become "American English." Indeed, Americans speak an English that has been changed and challenged by the languages of Native Americans and Africans, and every race or ethnic group that has settled here. Language is a collective memory that conserves the Past even as it contends with the new. Choppin understood profoundly the importance of recording an essential part of our history and evolution. Like the *Comptes-rendus*, Jules Choppin's poetry illustrates the creation and preservation of the unique and exceptional sound of Louisiana's voice, in both his Creole verse and, no less, in the elegant standard French of this eminent Louisiana poet.

—M. LYNN WEISS

---

[i] The Tintamarre is an archive created by Centenary College in Shreveport, Louisiana. Its collection includes works in all genres from francophone Louisiana. Its ambition is to make this literature available to teachers and students around the world. http://www.centenary.edu/french/about.html

[ii] Victor Séjour, "Le Mulâtre" *Revue des Colonies* (March 1837) Print. Victor Séjour, *The Jew of Seville* (1844) ["Diégarias"]. Trans. Norman Shapiro. Chicago: University of Illinois Press, 2002. Print. Victor Séjour, *The Fortune Teller* (1859) [*La Tireuse de cartes*]. Trans. Norman Shapiro. Chicago: University of Illinois Press, 2002. Print. Victor Séjour, *The Brown Overcoat* (1859). Trans. Pat Hecht. *Black Theater USA: Plays by African Americans, The Early Period, 1847–1938*. James Hatch and Ted Shine, eds., (New York: The Free Press, 1974) 25–37. Print.

[iii] M. Lynn Weiss. Introduction. *Creole Echoes: The Francophone Poetry of Nineteenth-Century Louisiana.* Trans. Norman Shapiro. Chicago: University of Illinois Press, 2003. Print.

[iv] Heidi Kim. "Excerpts from Old Solomon; or, A Slave Family in the Nineteenth Century." *Periodical of the Modern Language Association.* 125.3 (2010): 798–815. Print. Kim notes that Testut wrote the novel in 1858 during his sojourn in New York City. The novel was not published until 1872.

[v] To that end, *The Multilingual Anthology of American Literature: A Reader of Original Texts with English Translations* eds., Marc Shell and Werner Sollors, was published by New York University Press in 2000. This anthology collects fiction, non-fiction, literary and prosaic writing, pictographs by Americans from every part of the globe. One exceptional discovery was a slave narrative written in Arabic, "The Life of Omar Ibn Said" (1831): 58–73.

[vi] At the time, the racial term "Creole"—differing from the linguistic term—applied to those of European ancestry born in a European colony or former colony.

[vii] Although their relationship began as student to teacher, over time Choppin and Fortier became fast friends. A birthday tradition emerged between them. On each man's respective birthday, the other would compose and read aloud a poem written for that occasion only. Gil Choppin generously shared with us his knowledge of his ancestor's early life, in particular the details of the friendship between Jules Choppin and Alcée Fortier. Choppin and Fortier died in the same year, 1914.

[viii] Alcée Fortier, "French Literature in Louisiana," *Periodical of the Modern Language Association* 2 (1886): 31–60.

[ix] Ruby Van Allen Caulfield, *The French Literature of Louisiana* (New York: Institute of French Studies, Columbia UP, 1929) 64. In *Louisiana Studies,* Alcée Fortier does not give a date for the founding of the society but notes that the first volume of *Comptes-rendus* was issued in 1876.

[x] Edward Laroque Tinker, *Bibliography of the French Newspapers and Periodicals of Louisiana* (Worcester, MA: American Antiquarian Society, 1933) 13–14.

[xi] Charles Edwards O'Neill, *Séjour: Parisian Playwight from Louisiana* (Lafayette: Center for Louisiana Studies, University of Southwestern Louisiana, 1995) 1–2.

[xii] A serialized novel, *Die Geheimnisse von New-Orleans (The Mysteries of New Orleans)*, by a German immigrant, Baron Ludwig von Reizenstein, was published for the German-speaking audience in *Louisiana Staats-Zeitung* between 1854 and 1855. The novel explores (exposes) "deviant" sex in New Orleans, which includes black and white, and homosexuality. Indeed it may be the first published narrative of Lesbian love and sexuality in the United States. Ludwig von Reizenstein, "Lesbian Love." *The Multicultural Anthology of American Literature*, Marc Shell, Werner Sollors, eds. (New York: New York University Press, 2000) 185–209.

[xiii] Frans Amelinckx, "La Littéature louisianaise au xix siècle," *Présence francophone* 43 (1993) 15–17; Auguste Viatte, *Histoire de la Littérature de l'Amérique française des origines à 1950* (Paris: Presses Univeritaires, 1954) 298–299.

[xiv] Alcée Fortier, *Louisiana Studies: Literature, Customs and Dialects, History and Education* (New Orleans: F. F. Hansell, 1894) 64. *Comptes-rendus* was published between 1876 and 1951.

[xv] The Tintamarre archive at Centenary College published *Fables et Rêveries: Poésies*, a collection of Jules Choppin's poetry; ed., Roxanne Smith (Centenary College of Louisiana Press, 2007).

[xvii] Meschacébé is the French rendering of Mississippi, believed to mean the "father of waters." In nineteenth-century texts, the accenting of the name varied. According to *An Ojibwa Lexicon*, the word "Mississippi" is Ojibwa and means "big river."

[xviii] "Jean-Pierre Claris de Florian (1755–1794), French poet and playwright, author of fables generally considered second only in literary importance to those of La Fontaine. Choppin's version is, as expected, a very free adaptation." *Translator's note.*

Poems in Louisiana Creole

CIGALE ET FOURMI

Madame Cigale tout tempes olé chanter
    Et boire à la santé
Li pas jonglé l'hiver… li bien fou bin.
Pan ga, Cigale, ta manqué to di pain
Ain jour, li cou côté mamselle fourmi :
Li bordé li ; et dit li : « mon amie,
Baye moin, si ou plait, ain pai di pain,
    Ma rende vous li dainmain matin. »

« Pas d'ça, minette, ma pas prêté di pain :
Yé di : rende moun service baye moun chagrin,
    Et pis, to trop lainmain chanter ;
        Faut to travaille ain pé…
        Couri,… to trop fronté.
Si to travaille, quand gros l'hiver vini
Ta va gaingnain comme moin, fourmi,
    Di pain l'hiver, di pain l'été.
        Quittez metchié chanter
    Ça très mauvais pour la santé. »

I preserve the poet's syllabic indents where he clearly intends them, but do not presume to "correct" him where lines have too few or too many syllables. I also leave his occasionally erratic punctuation as is, except for obvious misprints.

GRASSHOPPER AND ANT

Madame Grasshopper all time do same thing:
    Dance and drink toast to health: "Clink clink"...
    But winter come... No song, no drink,
        Gone everything!
You see, Grasshopper! Bread go disappear!
One day she run next door, ask Ant: "My dear,
    Me beg... A little bread? Me pay
    You back tomorrow, break of day."

"No, no, mam'zelle! Me no bread-lender, me!
Man say: 'We suffer when we lender be.'
    You love sing song. That all you do.
    A little work better for you...
    Shoo! You got nerve, me tell you true!
If you work when big winter storm blow free,
Plenty be yours—like Ant!—believe you me!
    Bread winter and bread summer too...
    So, singing finish. Done! All through!
    Song bad for health, no good for you!"

Grasshopper: I purposely choose to translate *cigale* as "grasshopper," though "cicada" would be more correct, because I am told that it has that meaning in Louisiana Creole. As it is, English translations of the Aesopic original vary.

LE LOUP ET LA CIGOGNE

Michié Loup—gros—gavion li si content bafré
Qui li jamain gardé ça qui lapé mangé
Et li valé si tant gros bef avec zognon,
Qu'ain jour ain gros dézo croché dans so gavion.
Li té olé hélé mais li té pas capab.
Li commencé débat et li té per comme djab,
Alorse li prend so pate pou li fait signe Docter,
Et ça Docter la fait faut mo dit vous aster :
Docter la galopé (c'était ain vié zozo
Yé té pélé Cigogne) pou halé so dézo ;
Et li fouré so bec où dézo la rété,
Et sauvé la vie Loup comme ain bête qui li té.
Va oir cofaire et va conain comment Docters
Qui cou traité tout moun trompé dans yé zaffaires :
Pou ça li fait, gouloupia la té bien content
Mais quand Docter Cigogne té mandé li l'argent
Pou grand service li té baye li, coquin la dit :
« Ga, couri to chimin, zozo pate longue, couri,
To capab dit merci Bon Djé to sauvé to la tête. »
Et pauv Docter Cigogne couri comme ain vié bête.

THE WOLF AND THE STORK

"Fat-Gullet"—Wolf, him with big appetite—
Happy when eat a bunch, but him not bright:
Careless when chew… One day him swallow chunk
Of meat—with onion too! But look! Big hunk
Of bone get stuck! Him try to yell, but no,
No can make sound. Him struggle, strangle… Oh!
Poor devil scared. Him think him done for, dead!
So go wave paw up, down, all round by head,
Hope him make doctor come… Me tell you now,
Doctor—old bird, name Stork—come fast, and how!
She go stick beak down throat… Get bone, pull free,
Save life! But Stork big fool, believe you me!
Like Doctor who cure everybody, but
Get cheated… Have no head for business, what!
"Fat-Gullet" happy for what Stork she do,
But when she ask for pay, "You stupid, you!"
Sly Wolf him say. "Ha! Long-Legs, scoot! By heck,
You go thank God me let you save damn neck!"
And Stork so happy she escape Wolf's jaws,
Go running off like dumb old fool she was.

LA COLOMBE ET LA FOURMI

Ain jou, ain ti mamzel yé té pélé Colombe
Tapé promnain tout sel, côté bayou, dans l'ombe,
Là-bas en bas gros n'harbe, quand li oi dans do l'eau
Ain pauv piti fourmi, dibout, en hau ain copeau,
Et qui tapé débat pou sauver so la peau.
Colombe fait li signe, et di li tende, pas per…
Et cher ti nange la halé fourmi à ter.
Et ti fourmi, pauv djab, cou brassé so geounoux
Et pis, di li comme ça : « Mamzel mo lainmain vous ;
Ma rende vous ça ain jou, comme Bon Djé tendé moin,
Et mo va prende mo cœur pou jige et pou témoin. »
Et ça rivé comme li té dit. Colombe, ain jour,
En haut ain n'harbe dans bois tapé jonglé l'amour :
Et jiss quand li tapé chanter « chacaine so tour »,
Ain homme qui té la chasse, qui té fou bin fourmis,
Vizé mamzel Colombe, mais qui vous cré, zamis ?
Même ti fourmi la qué Colombe té sauvé,
Piqué talon n'homme la et ça fait li graté,
Li largué so fisi et li roulé par terre :
Tout so tracas rivé sans li connain cofaire ;
Et ti fourmi la dit : « Couri, mo ti zozo…
Ga li, ga li la-bas : li manqué so gombo.
— Merci, Colombe la dit, malé volé dans bois,
Mais avant ma parti, vini, molé bo toi. »

THE DOVE AND THE ANT

Little mam'zelle, name Dove, go promenade
One day, alone, by bayou. Stroll in shade
At foot great big tall tree, when, suddenly,
Out there on water, tiny ant she see—
Poor thing!—who stand on scrap, and, in big stir,
Struggle to save her skin. Dove wave at her,
Tell her: "Wait! You no be afraid!" And pull
Her quick to shore, like angel, merciful…
And ant, poor devil, make straight for her knees
And plant big kiss. Then say: "May good God please,
Me love you, friend! My heart, it tell you true,
Mam'zelle, one day me go do same for you!"
And, sure enough, it happen like she say.
Dove, high on treetop, sing for love one day.
And, when she say, "Soon be my turn to love,"
Hunter come, not give damn for ants, see Dove,
Aim at mam'zelle… But then, ah! What fine sight!
Ant—same one from before!—nip at him, bite
At heel… Shotgun go fly… Man scratch, man itch,
Go roll on ground—back, forth, fro, to—toss, pitch
Over and over, make big rumpus, heard
All round!… What now ant do? "You, dear friend bird,"
Him tell Dove. "Shoo! Escape! Bad man no take you
Now… No more never shoot you for to make you
His gumbo stew!" "Me fly," says Dove…" "Godspeed!…"
"But first, me thank you, friend, for such good deed!"

LE RENARD ET LA CIGOGNE

Ain jour au soir, Cigogne (mo cré c'était so fête)
Té invité Rénard soupé en tête à tête ;
Et vo conain Rénard gourmand, c'est pas pététe.
Michié Rénard rivé longtemps avant la nouit,
Et pis li tende tout sel jisqu'à dinain la tchouit.
« Bam-by » Cigogne vini, salué michié Rénard
Qui tout moun réconnaite pour ain famé vénard.
En haut la tab y avait ain jog, comme jog do l'eau Cologne.
Qui té gaingnain ain cou pli longue qué cou cigogne,
Madame parti mangé et li fouré so bec
Dans fond jog la, ma chère, et li netché li sec.
Et pis li di : « cofaire vo pas mangé, Rénard,
Vo ti la geole pointi, comme ain ti bec canard. »
Alorse qui ça va cré Rénard la fait,… dis moin,
Li jisse senti, tendé, et li parti colère ;
Li bat so jié, et mordé so la langue, ma chère.
Li liché so la lêve et cou assise dans coin :
Li oir madame Cigogne té gaignain so vente plein.
Li lévé so la tché tout dréte et li fou camp
Pasqué li té colère Cigogne fou li en d'dans.
Main c'est pas tout, couté, va oir comme li malin.
Avant parti, li dit : « Madame, vini dainmain matin,
Ma lé tende vous bon her, no va gaingnain boudin,
Saucisse et zandouillete, et tout ça vo lainmain. »
Et pis, à force li ri, li té manqué touffé,
Pasqué li té conain qui ça li t'allé fait.
Et qui vous cré, ma chère? Rénard di li vini,
Vini comme viés zamis, pas fait cérémonie.
Dinain té d'ja tout prête dans plat qui té tout plate :

THE FOX AND THE STORK

One night, Stork—birthday, maybe?—she invite
Fox (name Renard) come for have meal that night,
Just him, her… Well, no "maybe"! You be right
Think Fox him be big eater: him love stuff
Face full! So, him come early, sure enough,
Before be night, wait all alone, until
Him get big appetite, fit to go kill!…
By and by, Stork she come, tell him hello.
You bet Fox him be lucky so-and-so!
Table have jug—like for perfume, but tall—
And jug same shape as Madame Stork, by heck!
Why? Because it have long, thin, skinny neck…
Well, she stick beak down deep, go lap up all,
Every drop! Then she say: "M'sieu, how come
You no eat nothing? Oh, poor thing, by gum!
Too bad you dumb! You just no got much luck
With silly little mouth what look like duck!"
Now, tell me, what you think Renard him do?
Him furious mad, fit to be tied, but too
Smart for complain! So him bite tongue and think,
Run sit in corner, watch Stork drink and drink
Big belly full… Then, proud, him scoot—quick, quick! Him
Burn up for sure because damn Stork she trick him…
But that not all! Story not done. Oh, no!
Fox no be through… Before him up and go,
Him tell Stork: "Friend, tomorrow morning, come
My house, have meal. All dish you like… Yum-yum!
Blood pudding, sausage, tripe…" Then Fox him laugh
And laugh… Him almost burst, damn near go "paf'!"
Because him think what him go do… Him tell her:

C'était ain vié la soupe tout fréte sans ain patate.
Michié Rénard té faim, li liché sa lassiette,
Et pauv madame Cigogne té pas trapé ain miette.

"Come... No need for big frill... Me simple feller,
Us two old friend!" Next morning, table set:
Cold soup on platter... Flat... Food? Not one bit—
Potato? Nothing!... Stork stand, look at it...
Fox hungry, lick plate clean... And Stork? Ho-hum!
Madame, poor thing, no get one blessed crumb!

LE LOUP ET LE CHIEN

Ain jour gros papa chien contré pauv michié Loup
Plat comme ain pinaise et maig comme ain déclou,
À force gros chien layé ta pé guetté partout.
« Gros Boule, dit li, to sot, sorti dans bois,
Suive moin, to va content comme ain lé roi. »
Loup mandé Boule : « qui ça ma gain pou fait ?
— À-rien… manger, bafrer, boire café,
« Et guetter moun qu'a pé vini voler.
« Mo mait li bon, li va donne toi la crême,
« Pâtés pigeons, saucisses Jérisalem.
« Vini, ta oir, vié mait va lainmain toi.
« Ta fait comme moin, et ta blié dans bois. »
Yé tous les dés parti ; mais, tout d'ain coup,
Avant yé té rendi dans grand la cou,
Michié vente plat té oir la marque collier
Quand yé fermain gros Boule dans poulailler,
« Hey, ga, qui ça ça yé ? to cou corché »,
Vié Loup dit Boule quand yé ta pé marcher.
« A-rien. — Comment a-rien ? — C'est mo zaffaire.
— Quand-même, dis moin, molé connain cofaire.
— Ça to oir là, c'ain ti la marque collier
« Quand mo mait maré moin les soirs pou mo boyer.
— Qui ça ? yé maré toi ? ah bin michié lé roi,
« Ma pé dit vous adjé, ma pé fou camp dans bois.
    « Mo lainmain mié la Liberté,
    « Qui to la crême et to pâté. »

THE WOLF AND THE DOG

Fat papa dog him happen meet one day
Poor M'sieu Wolf. Him flat—like bedbug, say—
And thin like nail, from all big hound what chase him.
Dog—name Big Butch—him stop in track and face him:
"You stupid, spend all life in wood! Why you
No follow me and live like king, you too?"
Wolf ask: "Like king? But… What? How? What me do?"
"Nothing! You eat, stuff face, drink *cafè crème*,
Stand guard, watch out for thief, go bark at them…
My master, good man! Feed Jerusalem
Sausage, sweet cream, pigeon *pâté*… All kind
Fine thing! Him love you! Come, leave wood behind
For good, and make like me!" So off them go
To house… But suddenly, before you know,
Him with flat empty belly stop… Him holler:
"Wait!" And him point to mark where Butch have collar
When master chain him up in hen-house… "What…
What you got there on neck? There… What you got?…"
"Got? Nothing…" "Nothing?… Oh! That something! See?"
"What? Just small little mark when him chain me
At night, so me bark loud if robber come!"
"Chain you? You? King?… Me scram! Damn! Me no dumb!
        Back to wood! Freedom, night and day,
        Beat *cafè crème* and fine *pâté!*"

LE CHÊNE ET LE ROSEAU

Ain jour gros Chêne dit ti Roseau :
« To plis piti qu'ain ti zozo,
Ain ti di vent, pas plis, ma chère,
Capab d'ain cou fou toi par terre. »

« To bien hardi, gros n'harbe cochon,
To gros, mais faib comme ain mouton,
Attende di vent, ta oir, ma chère,
Qui moun qui va coucher par terre. »

Di vent vini, di vent soufflé,
Et tout d'ain coup li rédoublé ;
        Tchombo, roseau !…
        Roseau tchombo,
        Mais pour gros chêne
        Qui dans la plaine
        So feilles parti
        Li tout-tout ni.

Morale

Pas fait gros vente, ain jour ta vini plat ;
Gros papa lion ça peur ain ti dérat.

THE OAK AND THE REED

One day fat oak, him stand and talk
With little reed: "Wind come, go 'awk!'
You small like bird, so you know what?
Breeze blow, him knock you flat on butt!"

Reed, him say: "You brave, like fat pig,
But weak like lamb! Who care how big?
You wait... Wind come and, you know what?
We go see who fall flat on butt!"

Wind, him come blow and, not too long,
Sudden, him go blow twice as strong:
       Hold on, poor reed!...
       Poor reed hold on...
       But oak? Indeed!
       All nice leave gone,
       And him lay there,
       All bare, all bare.

Moral

Don't go make boast. One day you go lay flat:
Big papa lion get scared of little rat.

Entretien sur les 12 mois de l'année

Extraits

Par un vieux nègre st-jacquois nommé « Pa Guitin »

JANVIER

Pan ga, vié moun, panga ; vancé côté di fé ;
Fait fret déyor, entrez, et vini boi café ;
La plie apé tombé en'aut bêtes qui dans savane,
Nous autres, merci Bon Djé, nous gaingnain bon cabane.
Vini, piti, sorti dans fret… tendé di vent…
Vitement ! — Gagaye, mo fi, cou pélé to mouman,
Di li vini tout souit, li temps pou nous dormis ;
Di li, li pé rété trop tard chez so zamis.
Napé couri dans clos avant soleil lévé ;
Faut no couri dans fret quand même no doite crévé,
Nalé coupé di cane, nalé mangé sirop,
Vié neg l'habitation ça janmain gaingnain trop.
« Mangé, piti, mangé » (vié mait coutime di ça,)
« Jordi ta va gaingnain, dainmain ta gaingnain pas. »
Di gri avec sirop, c'est ça tout moun l'ainmain :
Mangé piti, et pis dormis jisqu'à dainmain,
Quand jou vini, dibout, comme si c'était l'été,
Si dormi trompé toi ta tendé fouet pété.

Chat on the Twelve Months of the Year

Excerpts

By an old black from Saint-Jacques by name of "Papa Guitin"

JANUARY

You, old folk, take good look. Outside me think
Be cold... Too cold... Come in. You sit and drink
Coffee by fire. In field, plenty rain fall
On animal—poor thing—and soak them all!
But us, thank God, got hut, so us keep dry.
You, young folk, hear wind blow! But, by and by,
Out you go—quick, quick!—out in cold! Go run
Tell *maman* she come home, no more have fun
With friends... Now time us sleep. But soon, before
Sun rise, time us run out and work some more!
In cold! No matter... We go freeze! Go cut
Down cane... Live on molasses, nothing but!
Old field black, on plantation, him so poor...
"Eat, eat... "old master tell him. "Yes, for sure,
Today you earn. Tomorrow? Nothing! So...
Grits and molasses... "Such fine feast!. Now, go
Eat, young folk, then go sleep. Come dawn, no stay
In bed... Up! Up!... Like on nice summer day.
But you sleep late, too long, lie flat on back,
And oh! You wrong! Pay price: Whip crack, go *clak*!

AVRIL

Ô ! rose du printemps qui fleuris sur les joues,
Qui ça n'homme-là pé dit ? coutez... mo cré li fou.
Toi dont le doux parfum embaume notre vie,
Pas rété côté li, couri piti, couri...
Emblême de beauté, d'amour et de délices,
Coutez, mo cré lapé dit quichose pou cribisses.
Je te revois encore, étoile de la terre,
Attende... pététe li faim... o pététe li colère.
Rosa, ton coloris prête un charme divin,
Mo cré li soif aussi, lapé parlé di vin.
Au front de la beauté, sur la joue de l'enfant,
Li sembe lapé crié... mo sir li pas content,
Tu règnes triomphante, ô reine des amours,
La pé jonglé so « gal» lalé chanter : « toujours, toujours »,
Toujours pour ta beauté tout mon amour éclate !
Jiss comme ti mait chanté, quand li sorti théiat,
Mais mo per li, malé, mo pas l'ainmain n'homme fou ;
Malé dans mo cabane... mo pas dans compte voudou.

APRIL

"O rose, bloom on the cheek, rose of the spring,"
—What that guy say? Listen... Him crazy thing!
"You, whose sweet scent perfumes us, every one..."
—Little one, no stay near him! Go! You run...
"Love's—beauty's—emblem, and joys they beget,"
—You hear? Him no make sense! Him nuts, you bet!
"I see you yet, fair star earth's labor bore."
—Wait... Maybe him be hungry... Maybe sore...
"Rosa, your hue bestows a charm divine"
—Or maybe thirsty... Him talk about wine?
"On beauty's brow, on children's cheeks as well... "
—See how him yell? Me sure him sore as hell!
"You reign triumphant! Queen of love, forever!"
—Him sing for girlfriend... Never stop! No, never!
"Ever my love springs from your beauty. Ah!"
—Like master... Him leave theater, sing "Tra-la..."
Him mad! Me go!... Him scare me, sure enough!
Stay safe in hut... No mix in voodoo stuff!

My punctuation attempts to clarify the original's dialogue in alternating
French and Creole.

MAI

Salouez, salouez, tout moun, nous autres dans mois la Vierge
Piti, couri l'église, couri limain vo cierge… !
Chantez cantique, chantez pou bon mouman Bon Djé,
Couri et bo so pied quand va di li adjé.
Quand mo té jène, mo té si tant lainmain l'église
Qué mo té chapé là quéquefois dans mo chimise,
Et mo té porté flers, tout nespèce flers dans bois,
Et pis mo té toujou content comme ain lé roi.
— C'est mois où ti zozo dja ponde yé ti dezef,
Où yé planté maïs pou milets, choual et bef,
Où souche l'année passée commencé marqué rang ;
C'est mois-là qué tout moun et tout quichose content.
Dezefs apé béqueté dans n'arbe, dans poulaillé,
Chapons mainnain poulets comme poule, vini oi yé.
Mais panga flève, gros flève, quand li parti gonflé
Yé tendé li roulé comme moun qu'apé ronflé,
Si li cassé lalvée, adjé maïs, adjé di cane,
Adjé fossé, barrière, jardin et pis cabane !
Tous zanimaux néyé, et mo ti mait fou camp…
La révini ain jou, mais Bon Djé conain quand.

38

MAY

Greeting to all! This, month of Virgin fair...
Little one, go run church! Light candle there!
Sing hymn mother of God, like time you tell
Her picture she be sure protect you well
When you go off... When me small child, me blessed,
Love church so much, sometime me go part-dressed,
And me go for pick flower in wood, and bring
All kind for her, so happy, me, like king.
—Now, month when little bird lay egg. when you
Plant grain for mule, and horse, and bull... When new
Shoot from last year begin push up and grow
All over—here, there. all in nice neat row.
Month when all people, thing, be happy; when
Egg in nest start go hatch, in tree, in pen;
When capon strut for chicken, like him hen,
Look them all up and down!... But month for be
Careful for river! Listen! Watch step! See
Water it go swell up... And more... And more...
And make big noise—you hear? Like man what snore...
If levee break, dam burst, and you know what?
Garden, corn, cane, bye-bye! And bye-bye hut!
Animal drown... Master save ass... Well, he
Come back some day. But God know when, not me.

JUIN

Hey, nos zamis ! fait chaud et tout moun allé soué,
Et c'est jiss en bas n'arbe qué ti moun capab joué.
Vié neg dans rang di cane apé tournain la terre
Avec yé la charrie, mais… phu !… yé pi la souère,
Quand yé sorti du bout yé rang, là-bas dans clos,
Yé tombé press par terre, pauv djab, à force yé chaud.
Longtemps quand mo té jène mo té content biché,
Et mo té fort comme d'jab pasqué mo té gauché,
C'est vrai : moun qui gauché toujours plis fort, yé dit.
Aster mapé posé, malé fermain mo jié,
Assise dans ma cabane, tout sel, pasqué mo vié.
— Des figues apé vini et ti zoranges aussi,
Raisins apé grimpé, grénades apé grossi,
Des oies, canards dans gros bayou pé barboté,
Poule apé ponde partout et coq apé chanté,
Et vive l'été, mo dit, malgré fait chaud comme djab,
L'été to capab prend la fraiche en bas ain n'arbe,
Mais quand di vend l'hiver soufflé en bas la porte
Tout moun parti colère et dit li « d'jab t'emporte. »

JUNE

Hey, friend! It real hot now, and everyone
Sweat big. Kid play round tree, in shade, have fun...
Old black plow earth in row of cane, and when,
Later, them get to end, whew! So hot, then,
Almost go fall on ground, poor thing! Them not
Like me when me young man... Never too hot,
Love work, and me strong devil, every day...
Why? Because me left-handed, and man say
Left hand more strong than right. But now, all my
Time, only sit in cabin, doze, close eye...
Why? Because now me old. What more can do?
—Soon, fig on tree, and soon have orange too...
Grape climb up vine, and pomegranate grow
Big, full... Goose, duck splash round bayou... Cock crow
And hen go lay egg here and there. Me yell:
"Hurrah for summer!" Who care hot as hell!
Plenty shade under tree! Nice, cool... Go sit...
But when wind blow in winter, when hear it
Creep under door, people get mad, cry: "Oh!
To hell with you, you goddamn so-and-so!"

SEPTEMBRE

Li temps pou fait di foin, li temps halé di bois.
Que dit ce pauvre noir dans son affreux patois?
N'homme là semblé comme si li tolé fout dé moin.
Il a parlé, je crois, du temps, de bois, de foin.
Panga li parlé moin, o ma fou li par terre.
Sa voix a retenti de rage et de colère.
Où djab n'homme là sorti ? et qui ça lapé dit ?
Dans sa colère immense, ah ! m'aurait-il maudit ?
Y faut mo parlé li pou conain ça li olé.
Et de le voir ainsi mon âme est désolée.
Bon Djé qui ça ça yé ? malé séyé chapé,
Quelque esprit infernal, hélas, l'aura frappé...
Mais non, faut mo vancé, mais, pas vancé trop proche.
Peut-il, sur moi, passant, me lancer un reproche ?
Malé dit vous la vérité : mo per n'homme là...
Pourqoui me craindrait-il ? Il semble fuir... holà...
Pardon, michié, mais mo pressé,... malé dans clos.
Il part, je reste seul ; il me tourne le dos.
Quitté mo galopé ; piti, cou côté vo mouman.
Il ne connaît ce noir, ni souci, ni tourment.
Si mo té pas per li, mo srait donne li gombo.
Hélas, mourir ainsi qu'il serait doux et beau !
Mo té conain li fou... lapé parlé pou bo.
À l'ombre du Sachem dormir dans un tombeau.
Qui... moin bo so ladgeole ? adjé, malé dans clos.

42

SEPTEMBER

"Time for make hay. Time for chop wood, go fetch…"
—That vile patois! What can he mean, black wretch?
"Him there… Make fun… Him treat me like no good!"
—I thought I heard him mention time, hay, wood…
"Him watch tongue, or me knock on ass! Him see!
—What rage rings in his voice! Is it for me?
"Goddamn! Where him come from? What him say? Oh!…"
—Such temper! Did he curse me? Who's to know?
"Maybe me talk… See what him have in head…"
—His anger leaves me quite dispirited!
"God! What kind man them be? Better me run?
—Is he possessed by some Infernal one?
"Maybe me go stand talk… But no too near…"
—What now? Is he about to taunt and jeer?
"Me tell you true, him scare me. Him cuckoo!"
—What? Does he fear me? Is he leaving?… You!…
"Pardon, m'sieu. Me hurry. No can stay."
—Wait!… Now he turns to go… You there… I say…
"Me run!… You, little one, run find mamma…"
—Ah! What a simple life! Care? Torment? Bah!
"If me no scared, me cook him gumbo stew!
—And death itself? Alas! How easy too…
"What? See? Him crazy! Him think that be true!
—Entombed forever in his Sachem's view…
"Who? Him think him go trap me? Bye! Me through!"

_____

Regarding my punctuation of alternating lines, see p. 37.

LA CHASSE CHAOUÉ

Vo cré malé menti! À bin... Ça malé dit
Si c'est pas vrai, ma chère, molé mouri jordi.
Ain jour, moin et ti mait no parti cou la chasse,
Et no mainnain nos chiens pou yé té suive la trace
Chaoué, là bas dans bois. Ti mait prend so fisi,
Et moin mo prend... jiss dévinain ça mo soizi...
Un gros papa bâton assez pou tchoué ain lours
(Si lours là pas trop gros pou fait mo prend la course,)
No parti grand matin... (nous autres c'est « 'fore day coon »)
Et quand no cou la chasse, no pas fait comme tout moun :
Prémier qui chose qué no contré là-bas dans bois
C'était chaoué, la djeole pointi et ti jié nois.
Li parti galopé, mais tayo té oir li,
Mo mait et moin no té oir li passé aussi,
Et no bardé derrière chaoué... Vo parlé pou lapin,
Yen pas lapin qui galopé comme mo ti mait et moin.
No rivé tink à tink derrière compère chaoué
Et no baissé pou trapé so la tché... a-ouay !
Vite comme ain l'éclair li chapé dans ain trou.
À for mo té pressé mo tombé en'aut mo geounou.
Trou la té dans racine ain n'harbe au ras la terre,
Mo té oi li entré dans trou, mais par malher,
En'aut l'aute côté n'harbe là yen vé ain l'aute gros trou,
C'est par trou-là qué li chapé pou fout dé nous.
Ti mait dit moin: « fourré to bras et trapé li... »
Mais chia! bête-là té loin, bête-là té djà parti.
Mais no té pas conain, ni mon ti mait ni moin,
Et no té cré, qué no té cernain-li dans coin.
Mo roulé mo la manche et mo graté la terre
Comme poules quand yolé ponde, o chiens quand yé colère.
Aster qui ça vo cré mo taté dans trou là
Pendant ti mait tapé hélé « houra, houra. »
Ain gros qui chose qui té tout fret et qui té rond,

THE RACCOON HUNT

I bet you no believe and think me lie!...
Well, if me no tell true, me hope go die,
Here, now... So! One day, me go with young master
Out for hunt. Take dog, so them chase, go faster,
Faster, when sniff out track... Master him take
Shotgun, and me... You guess? No make mistake!
Me grab big stick—papa stick sure enough!—
Good for kill bear (if bear him no too tough
Or come run after!)... Well, just like me say,
Master and me, before sun-up that day,
Go off for hunt... Us two, believe you me,
No hunt like other folk... What first thing be
Cross path in wood? Raccoon! Have beady eye
And pointy snout... Fat as you please, shoot by...
Him gallop! Fly! But me and master too,
When see him there, do like what rabbit do...
No! Even rabbit no so fast! And soon,
Master and me catch up with friend raccoon.
Then bend down, think pick up... But when get near,
Make grab, him fast like lightning, disappear
In hole in ground, and me fall down, go splat!
Well, right near hole, big tree trunk—hollow, flat—
And me see 'coon run in, so think now me
Can catch... But damn! On other end me see
Other big hole, and sure enough him jump
In that one now, so one two three him dump
Master and me! And master tell me: "Go
Stick arm in... Pull him out!" But no one know
Him make escape, run off... So me go round,
Roll shirtsleeve up and me start scratch at ground
Like dog when him get good and mad, or hen
When she lay egg... And when me ready, then
Me go reach hand in hole and... Oh la la!
While master watch and yell "Hurrah! Hurrah!"

Et quand ti mait dit moin: « taté plis loin, plis fond,
« Mettez to dé la main, Guitin, pas per fouillé... »
Mais mo té djà senti bête-là apé grouillé ;
Et quand mo dit mo mait : «mo per, malé fou camp »,
No oi l'aute côté n'harbe ain gros papa serpent
Qui lévé so la tête quand li sorti dans trou...
Et c'est la vérité ça mapé conté vous :
Quand mo oi so lancette mo manqué tournain fou.
Mo mait li té pas per et li tiré bête-là ;
Aster c'était mon tour pou mo hélé « houra ! »
So gros la tête sauté comme ain ti graine tac-tac ;
Mo ramassé bête-là et fourré li dans sac.
Et quand no révini la chasse no tapé soué,
Ea pis tout moun ri nous pou no la chasse chaoué.

Épilogue

Aster, pauve chiens leyé tapé dormi dans coin,
Yé té rivé longtemps avant mo mait et moin.
Mo sir qué quand yé oi c'était serpent sonnettes
Yé bardé la maison, yé té trop per, pauve bêtes.

You no believe what thing me feel! Round, big,
Cool skin... And master more him shout: "Dig! Dig!
More, more, Guitin! No be afraid! Both hand..."
But me already feel thing wriggle, and
Me say: "No! Me no stay! Me scared! Me run!"
Just then me see come out from tree trunk one
Goddamn big snake! When lift head up, uncurl
By hole, bare fang, me scared, damn near lose mind!
Really! No lie!... Now master him show how
Be brave. My turn go yell "Hurrah!"... See? Now
Him take gun, aim, shoot snake in big fat head,
And "pow!" like little seed pod... Snake fall dead...
Me pick up, stuff in pack. When get back, soon,
People make fun how we two hunt raccoon!

Epilogue

Over in corner, dog them sleep. Them get
Back home in plenty hurry you can bet!
Finish hunt long before master and me:
Them no want mess with rattler, no sirree!

L'HUÎTRE ET LES PLAIDEURS

Dé n'hommes tapé promnain, ain jou, au bord la mer.
Yé tous les dés ensemble oi ain dézouite parter.
Ain dans yé happé li, et dit c'était pou li...
L'aute la té si colère qué li talé fou li,
Mais jige la galopé pou péché yé té bat,
Pasqué dé n'hommes léyé té là comme chien et chat.
Et li dit yé : « ouzaute sorti trouvé dézouite,
« Attende, et ma dit vous pou qui li yé... tout souite. »
Li ouvri dézouite la et pis li calé li ;
Et pis li dit : « comme main c'est jige, mo valé li.
« Et pis pou pas vou cré qué moin c'est ain canaille,
« Mapé donne vous chacaine ain joli ti lécaille. »

Morale

Si tolé dispité pas couri côté jige,
Pasqué ya oté toi jisqu'à to vié chimige.
Tout ça to capab fait yé va dit to coupab ;
Vaut mié to paix, et pis... débate comme to capab.

48

THE OYSTER AND THE ADVERSARIES

Two friend go walk one day by water, see
Oyster on ground, same time… One say: "That be
For me!" and go make grab… Other, him so
Angry, him say: "Oh?" Ready come to blow…
Then judge come by, run up, and him say: "Drat!
No need you two go fight like dog and cat!
Me know you just find oyster. But do better
Wait, and me tell you who, which one go get her…"
Then him crack oyster, swallow, one two three,
And say: "Me judge, so oyster be for me!
But me no want you think me snake from hell,
So here! Me give each one nice oyster shell."

Moral

Never ask judge decide! Judge all got knack
Steal everything, even old shirt off back!
Always you lose, no matter what. So then,
Better make peace… Later, go fight again.

LES SINGES ET LE LÉOPARD

Adaptation en patois créole d'une fable par Florian

Ain jour ain bande macacs tapé joué en bas n'abe
Là-bas dans bois, ensemble. Yé tapé ri comme djabe,
Et, ça yé tapé joué, c'était... plié yé dos,
Et tchombo yé la tête dans jambe ain vié macac
Qui semblé ain vié mam qui té fait yé dodo
Pendant qué yé la main té plate en haut yé dos.
Et, dans yé ti la main, chacaine té donné ain clac,
Et récuilé, roulé par terre comme moun qui chac.
Et tous macacs lé yé en ba nabe parti ri
Yé tapé joué, dansé, sauté, poussé des cris,
Quand tout d'ain coup, ma chère, yé oir ain léopard
Avec so gros la djole. Yé tous té per... dardard,
Li vancé côté yé, et li dit yé : « pas per,
« Pas per, pitits macacs... ga ! mo pas en colère ;
« Mo sorti réveiller, et mo tendé di bris,
« Et mo vini pou jouer avec ouzautes, pitits.
« À là moin, anon jouer : Baissez, macac... » et pim !
Bête la fou li ain clac... (esquisez mo la rime).
Di sang parti couler... yé tous fait semblant ri,
Mais li, li ri bon tchor. Yé tous parti couri
Dans tous façons chimins, dans bois, pasqué yé té conain
      Qui moun qui té cognain.

THE MONKEYS AND THE LEOPARD

A Creole patois adaptation of a fable by Florian.

Monkey troupe make big noise by tree one day
In wood. Like little devil, laugh and play
Together, clap hand, bash and bang and slap...
Old ape, like mammy, have one there on lap,
Little one, holding tight, like when you keep
Rocking, rocking, and try for make go sleep.
But look! Same monkey... Always little one,
Hunched up, all time get hit. Ho ho! Big fun!
Other dance, laugh, go roll about on ground,
Play, shout, have fine old time. Jump all around...
But oh, my dear! Sudden, so near, them see
Leopard! Fat jaw! Them scared, scared as can be...
And him come closer, closer... "Please," him say,
"Monkey friend, no be so afraid! Nay, nay!
Me no be angry! Me wake up just now,
Hear noise, come play. So, let's!... "Then, pow!
Him give good swipe at one... (Oh my, me make
Terrible rhyme! So? Sorry for mistake...)
Anyway, blood flow free. Monkey try smile,
Pretend be funny... Laugh... "Hee hee!" But while
Leopard him laugh from gut, all, one by one,
Monkey troupe up and into wood go run,
Here, there, every which way... Leopard, him show them
    Best monkey stay with friend what know them!

Morale

« Coutez moin, mo zamis, pas jouez avec "big-bock,"
« Pasqué ya griffé toi et porté toi bad lock.
« Yé va donne toi di sic, et pi yé va bo toi,
« Mais panga yé la djole ; ya mordé toi, quéquefois. »

Moral

So listen, you no play game with 'big buck!'
Paw turn to claw, and you get big bad luck!
Watch out! Them give you sugar word, but might
Come open jaw up wide and take good bite!

Florian: Jean-Pierre Claris de Florian (1755–1794), French poet and play-wright, author of fables generally considered second only in literary impor-tance to those of La Fontaine. Choppin's Creole version is, as expected, a very free adaptation.

LE LIÈVRE ET LA TORTUE

Raconté par « Pa Guitin »

Ain jou, compère Lapin et pis madame Torti
Lévé avant soleil. Yé té jonglé sorti
Pou cou assise au ras chimin pou yé posé,
Et comme dé vié zamis yé commencé causé.
Torti la dit Lapin : « qui ça tolé parlé
Ma rendi côté bit dans grand chimin, prémier ? »
Lapin la parti ri et dit Torti : « to fou…
Pou qui to prend Lapin, vié barbotère la boue ? »
Torti réponde : « an-hant, to per parié toujou…
To jis conain jonglé o-bin mangé di chou. »
« À-bin, top, ma parié », Lapin la dit… « Coupez »…
Et Torti la parti. Lapin la cou coucher,
Et pis sauter, danser, et berdasser longtemps.
Li té si sir gaingnain qué li té prend so temps.
Mais vié madame Torti marché *goudou, goudou,*
Pendant qué ti Lapin taé jouer comme ain ti fou ;
Et *zing* Lapin parti, mais li parti trop tard,
Et dans la monte Torti, Lapin té en rétard.

Morale

Zamis, coutez moin bien : quand volé fait quichoge
Faut vos lévé bonne her, et pis coûté l'horloge…
Sitôt li sonain *ting*… bardez, zamis, parti…
Va fait, pas comme Lapin, mais comme madame Torti.

THE HARE AND THE TORTOISE

Told by "Pa" Guitin

One day, before sun up, friend Rabbit come
Join Madame Turtle. Them decide, by gum,
Better them stay by path, poke round a bit,
Take easy Them old friend, and so go sit,
Have chat. .. Turtle she say to Rabbit: "See?
Little hill there, on road? Who bet—you, me,
Go race—me get there first!" "Ha hal Ho ho!"
Rabbit him laugh. "You crazy so-and-so!
Lazy old stick-in-mud! Me rabbit! Bah!
What you think rabbit do?" Turtle say: "Ha!
You scared you lose! You only good for play,
And for go nibble cabbage every day!"
"Oh?" Rabbit answer. "Good! Me bet!... You start!... "
So Turtle she begin... Rabbit him dart
Back, forth... Lie down, take nap... Get up, no hurry...
Jump, dance, do jig... Take plenty time... No worry,
Know easy him go win!... Turtle she walk
While silly Rabbit play... *Plok plok, plok plok...*
Then *whish!*... Him start up... Fly... Reach hill... Too late!
Turtle already there, just sit and wait!

Moral

Me give advice, friend. You got stuff to do?
When clock go off—*dring dring!*—you go off too!
If chance come for you win, better you grab it:
Go do like Madame Turtle, no like Rabbit.

LES ANIMAUX MALADES DE LA PESTE

Ain jou, pauve zanimaux tombé malade partout :
Milet dans la savanne, choual, chaoué, mitou,
Zozo dans bois, et cocodri dans grand bayou.
      Gros Lion ouvris so gros ladjole
      Et li parlé comme mait l'école.
Li dit yé tous : « Zamis, mo cré Bon Djé colère ;
« Y faut fait queq quichoge, o bin, queq la prière
« Avant no tous couri dans trou en bas la terre.
« Malé dit vous la vérité, comme moin c'est Lion.
« Mo déjà mangé cabri, chévreuil et plein mouton ;
« Mo dévoré yé tous sans yé fait moin à-rien,
« Et mo senti aster qué mo té pas fait bien.
« Et pis, pou ain quichoge faut mo mandé pardon :
« C'est pou n'homme la, pauv djab, qui té gardé mouton ;
« Mo mangé li tout comme les autes. Aster, coûté :
« Y faut tout moun vancé pou dit la vérité. »
Coquin Rénard la dit : « Abin… qui ça ça yé ?
« Chiah 1 [sic] tout ça c'est pas péché divant Bon Djé !
«Yé tous té doit content qué Lion té mangé yé. »
      Tout moun saloué et bat la main ;
      Yé srait fait ça jusqu'à dainmain,
Mais lours vini, gros lours, gros tig, chien, chat, tchoureil,
        Lapin, chévreil,
        Chaoué, lablette,
        Tout façon bête…
        Yé tous dit Lion
        Té gain raison.
Après tout ça, bourique, pauve vié bourique vancé
(Bon Djé conain qué c'était pas pou li dansé.)
Li dit : « ain jou mo té passé au ras chimin,
« Mo mangé ain pé zherbe queq moun mo pas conain. »

THE ANIMALS ILL WITH THE PLAGUE

One day, all animal get sick: mule who
Live on savanna, horse, raccoon, cat too,
Bird in wood, crocodile in big bayou...
    Lion, him open wide fat jaws,
    Explain, like teacher, why, what cause.
Tell them all: "Friend, me think good God him be
Angry... Some reason... So, believe you me,
Better go pray, confess, or, one two three,
Us all wind up down hole in ground! Me know,
Because me Lion, king! And so, me go
Talk first, and tell you truth... Lots time me kill
Goat, roebuck, sheep. Oh, plenty! Eat my fill,
Even though them no bother me! But now
Me know what awful thing that be. And how!
But me ask pardon for much worse me do:
Because man who watch sheep? Me eat him too!
So now, time everyone confess. All sinner..."
"But," answer Fox, "if them King Lion's dinner,
Them glad! Big honor, God above! Them winner!"
    Everyone clap, clap, clap... Would cheer
    Until tomorrow. But then, here
Come bear. And him stand there, confess... Big, fat...
        Then dog, then cat,
        Rabbit, raccoon
        Tiger, deer... Soon
        Squirrel and roach...
        All kind approach
And say King Lion right. Each one confess
Terrible sin... At last, old Ass she get
Up on her feet—no for dance minuet,
Good God, you bet!—and say: "One day, me go
Past field some stranger own... Me hungry! Oh,
So hungry... And me chew small blade of grass..."

« Qui ça to dit ? to volé zherbe ? attende bourique…
« Vancé tout moun… faut nous fouli des coup-t-labrique. »
Yé sommain li et roulé li comme ain barique.

Morale

    Si to riche, ya dit toi :
    « To vanyant comme le roi. »
    Si to pauve, mo piti,
    Divant jige to fouti.

"You what?" them other shout, and fall on Ass,
Beat her and pound her, throw poor thing on ground,
Alas! Like barrel, roll her round and round.

Moral

> You be rich, like king? For sure,
> Never crime, how bad you do.
> But, dear friend, if you be poor,
> Judge him say: "You done! Go screw!"

Poems in French

L'HOMME QUI EST DANS LA LUNE

Au bayou St-Jean

Dans le calme des nuits cet homme nous regarde ;
Du haut du firmament il nous dit: « prenez garde ! »
Celui qui fuit dans l'ombre ou rôde autour de vous,
N'est qu'un avant-coureur de bandes de filous :
Soyez prudents, fermez vos portes, vos fenêtres
Contre les attentats de ces ignobles êtres.
C'est pour que vous soyez à l'abri de ces gueux
Que je verse d'en haut mes rayons lumineux.
Ne vous fiez pas trop à l'homme de police :
Souvent il perd de vue un voleur qui se glisse.
"On dit qu'on a vu même," oh ! comble de malheur,
Ces gardiens de la paix dans la peau du voleur.
Saluez donc, amis, ma demeure argentine
Qui répand sur vos pas sa lumière divine,
Je suis plus important avec mes yeux d'Argus,
Pour vous et vos enfants, que la belle Vénus. »

THE MAN WHO IS IN THE MOON

At Bayou Saint-Jean

In the night sky he watches us. "Beware!"
He warns us from the heavens' height. "Take care!
That one who runs into the shadows, and
Who lurks about you there, heralds a band
Of roving thugs... Careful! Be sure to close
Your windows, doors, lest you fall prey to those
Ignoble creatures! For, indeed, if I
Cast down my beams of light from here, on high,
It is to spare you from fell consequence.
Even police offer no sure defense
Against such kind: often the thieves outrun
Those guardians of the peace, leave them outdone...
At times, one even sees—Oh, the chagrin!—
Those minions of the law in felons' skin!
So, friends, hail this my dwelling, silver-bright,
That spreads before your feet its heavenly light.
An Argus thousand-eyed, more do I do
Than Venus fair for all your kin and you."

ASSIS AU BORD DU BAYOU

Là-bas, à l'horizon, je vois le beau Phébus
Qui s'en va tristement en regardant Vénus.
Il se glisse, se glisse, en descendant dans l'ombre,
Dans l'ombre des grands bois, là-bas dans la nuit sombre,
Il dirigeait ses pas, seul et silencieux,
Vers l'espace infini, profond, mystérieux.

Son regard flamboyait de rage et de colère
D'avoir vu tout le jour tant de maux sur la terre :
Dès l'aube, il avait vu l'orphelin opprimé,
L'esclave dans les fers, l'imposteur acclamé…
Il s'écriait: « Mon Dieu, que de maux en ce monde !
Il n'est pas étonnant que ton tonnerre gronde.
Seigneur, laisse tomber un voile sur mon front ;
Je ne puis regarder l'insolence et l'affront.
Frappe donc, ô mon Dieu, dans ta juste colère,
L'*ingrat*, ce monstre affreux qu'a vomi sur la terre
Ce grand *maudit* de Dieu, l'infâme Belzébut
Il est là, ce *Damné*, comme un lion à l'affût.
Quand soudain il s'élance et qu'il saisit sa proie,
Tout l'enfer retentit d'allégresse et de joie.
Il souffle la vengeance au milieu des humains ;
Le meurtre l'accompagne, et le poignard en mains,
Il s'avance dans l'ombre : il se cache, l'infâme,
Pour frapper sa victime et lui ravir son âme. »

Sa place est aux enfers ; qu'il y reste à jamais,
Pour que l'homme ici-bas soit libre désormais.

SITTING BY THE BAYOU

On the horizon, fair Phoebus I see,
Gliding, gliding down into shade, as he
Sadly gazes at Venus as the high
Trees cast their shadows on the darkened sky.
He traced his path, alone and mute, where it
Led to the deep, mysterious infinite.

His glance flared red with raging anger, for
All day had he seen earth teem more and more
With ills: at dawn he saw the orphan child
Oppressed; the slave in chains; mankind beguiled
By charlatans… He cried: "My God, no wonder
That you growl at the world, peeling your thunder
For woes untold. My Lord, pray veil my eyes.
I cannot bear to watch the daylight rise
Over insult and insolence. Strike dead,
O God, in your just wrath, the monster bred
Of vomit puked by Beelzebub! Yes, strike
The monster down, accursed, who, lurking like
A lion at the ready, stalks his prey,
And who, seizing it, hears a loud 'hooray'
Rise from hell's fulsome precincts, and whose breath
Huffs and puffs vengeance; vows man's shadowed death,
Dagger in hand; stealthy, creeps to his goal,
Strikes, kills his victim, and purloins his soul."

Hell is his home; let it forever be,
So that man here below be ever free.

Phoebus: Phoebus is another name for Apollo, the Greek god of the sun,
who rode his golden chariot across the sky each morning.

Puis à l'autre horizon je vois « Phébé la blonde »
Qui commençait, le soir, son éternelle ronde.
Elle me voit assis au bord du vieux bayou,
Et me crie en passant : « Va te coucher, voyou. »

Then, on the near horizon, rises fair
Phoebe, starting her endless round up there,
Who sees me by the old bayou, and who
Sneers as she grazes past: "Go to sleep, you..."

N'EN DOUTEZ PAS

Lorsque sur mon chemin, un pauvre vieil ami
Me tend la main, et dit : « Je suis mort à demi,
« J'entends le cliquetis des ciseaux de la Parque,
« Et Caron qui me crie ; "allons, allons, embarque," »
Je me demande si, là-bas, dans le ciel bleu
Mon ami n'aura pas, un jour, tout près de Dieu
Sa place réservée. Où serait la justice
Si l'on n'était admis, après un long supplice,
À jouir du bonheur qu'on nous promet là-haut,
Et que nous attendons tôt ou tard, tard ou tôt.
Parce que nous vivons reclus et sans ressources,
Sans le moindre denier aux tréfonds de nos bourses,
Pourrions-nous un instant douter de la bonté
D'un Dieu qui nous appelle à son Éternité ?
Non, non, il nous dira dans sa juste clémence,
Ce Dieu : « Venez, enfants, voici la récompense
Que je gardais ici, pour vous, dès votre enfance ;
Entrez au Paradis… à droite… par ici…
Allez… comme eux là-bas, soyez anges, aussi. »

NO DOUBT ABOUT IT

When some poor friend stops me, from days gone by,
Holds out his hand and says: "Half dead am I...
I hear the clicking shears of murderous Fate
And Charon's cry: 'Come aboard... It grows late!'"
I ask myself if, in that sky of blue,
My friend will not, one day, have his place too
Beside the Lord. What kind of justice would
It be if, after life's travail, we should
Not be allowed to taste the happiness
Of heaven's realm, long promised us? Ah yes,
Sooner or later... What? Doubt that the Lord
Will share with us Eternity's reward,
Simply because we live—paupers or worse—
Without a blessèd penny in our purse?
No, no. This God, in his just clemency,
Will tell us: "Come, my children... Come, join me
In Paradise. This is the guarantee
I gave you in your youth. Yes, come this way...
Step to the right, my friends... Enter, I pray...
And, like all those you see, those others who
Stand yonder there... Come and be angels too."

Charon: Charon, in Greek mythology, is the boatman who ferries souls across the River Styx to Hades.

QU'EST-CE QUE L'ÂME ?

Dites-moi, dites-moi, ce que c'est que cette âme,
Ce fluide de vie, cette subtile flamme
Qui parcourt tout notre être et ne s'envole enfin
Que lorsque Dieu l'appelle ; elle est, dit-on, sans fin,
Et ne s'éteint jamais, cette flamme immortelle,
Qui descend parmi nous de la voûte éternelle.
Quel est ce feu subtil qui se glisse partout
Et qui nous fait mouvoir, et qui nous fait surtout
Penser, croire et douter. Dieu seul peut vous le dire ;
Son regard doux et bon dans un divin sourire
Remplit nos cœurs d'amour ; c'est l'écho de sa voix,
C'est son dernier soupir qui descend de la croix,
Voilà l'âme, ô mortels, cette perle divine,
Que Dieu créa, mais que le juste seul devine.

WHAT IS THE SOUL?

Tell me, what is it, this substanceless flame,
This subtle, living fluid with the name
Of "soul", that permeates our being and ever will
Remain within, never take flight, until
God calls it to his bosom? Limitless,
Endless, they say, this fire of timelessness,
Burning but everlasting, that descends
Upon us from the vault of heaven, but spends
Itself not out; force through our bodies spread,
That gives life to our limbs, thoughts to our head,
That makes us think, believe, and doubt?... Ah, but
God alone, only God can tell you what
It is; his glance, that smile divine of his
That, tender, fills our hearts with love... It is
The echo of his sigh—his last!—as he
Descends the cross... Yes, that, assuredly,
That is the soul, O mortals! Pearl divine,
God-wrought: none but the just plumb its design.

ENCORE LE VIEUX BAYOU

Souvent vers ce bayou je dirige mes pas,
Et là, je viens m'asseoir comme les grands-papas
Lorsque la jambe frêle et l'épine dorsale
Se ploient devant Thémis, la déesse impartiale.
Ensuite je me dis, tout en rêvant là-bas,
Tout en humant le soir ma pipe et mon tabac :
« Salut, Orion, salut, constellation divine,
Qu'admirèrent jadis et Ptolémée et Pline,
Toi que la chaste Diane a placé dans les cieux,
De ton éclat divin, Orion, remplis mes yeux ;
Je veux te contempler, sourire à ta lumière ;
Je veux un jour… un jour… à mon heure dernière
Adresser au Seigneur cette unique prière :
« Mon Dieu, puisqu'ici-bas Orion me fait veiller,
Qu'il soit au moins là-haut mon dernier oreiller. »

AGAIN THE OLD BAYOU

Often I turn my steps toward this bayou,
And sit, as our grand-papas used to do
When, frail of leg, back bending, they would bow
Before Themis, impartial goddess... Now,
I tell myself, dreaming of things up there,
Puffing my pipe-smoke blowing on the air:
"Greetings, Orion, godly constellation,
Whom Ptolemy's and Pliny's admiration
Glorified... You, whom fair Diana, chaste,
In bygone days, into the heavens placed;
Orion, fill my eyes with that divine
Blaze of your being. For I would, smiling, gaze
On your light... And I would, when done my days...
I would, at my last hour, my one prayer raise:
'Dear Lord, since long I watched him, comforted,
Pray, on Orion let me rest my head...'"

Themis: Less well known than the several other classical characters in this poem—historical and mythological—Themis was the Greek Titan goddess of divine law and order.

LES CLOCHES, AU BAYOU

Je les entends de loin ces cloches, au bayou ;
Elles semblent me dire à l'aube : *Oh! how are you ?*
« Levez-vous, paresseux, et venez à l'église,
Donnez le bras à Jeanne, à Laure, ou bien à Lise,
Et puis, à deux genoux, dites à Dieu : *Do please*,
Ô vous qui regardez dans le fond de mon cœur,
Venez à mon secours, et faites-moi l'honneur
De me dire ou de Jeanne, ou de Laure, ou de Lise,
(Sans trop vous occuper si ma moustache est grise)
À laquelle je dois, en tombant à genou,
Dire du fond du cœur: *I love you, I love you.*
Je suis dans l'embarras, un embarras extrême,
De savoir qui des trois est bien celle que j'aime. »

Le matin je me dis : « Mais c'est Jeanne, vraiment,
Car c'est bien elle, hélas ! qui cause mon tourment.
Le soir ce n'est plus ça ; c'est Lise que j'adore,
Ou bien Laure… que sais-je… Ô vous, vous que j'implore,
Dieu de bonté, venez, venez à mon secours ;
Veuillez me présenter l'objet de mes amours. »

        Tu n'es rien qu'un hibou
        En plein jour, vieux gribou ;
Ne vois-tu pas, bêta, que Lise, Laure, et Jeanne
        Ne font de toi qu'un âne ?

THE BELLS, IN THE BAYOU

Far off, I hear dawn's bells in my bayou;
They seem to say: "You, *comment allez-vous?*
Lazy! Get up and come to church! Give one
Of the three demoiselles—Laure, Lise, or Jeanne—
Your arm... Give her your arm and come this way...
And, when you do, fall to your knees and pray
The Lord above: 'O dear God, *s'il te plaît,*
Thou who seest in my heart, I beg thee please
To help me! Is it Jeanne, or Laure, or Lise?
(What difference, now that my mustache is gray!)
Tell me, to which one should I, kneeling, say:
"I love you. *Je vous aime, mademoiselle!*"
What a dilemma! Which one should I tell?'"

Come morn, I tell myself: "For sure, it's Jeanne.
Yes, she's the one who strikes me down, undone."
At night, Lise is the one I give my heart...
Or Laure?... Which?... Lord, thou who the true God art,
I beg thee, God of goodness, God above,
Help me please! Tell me which one do I love?"

      Look at yourself, old owl,
        You and your graybeard's scowl!
Can't you see that all three—Laure, Lise, Jeanne too—
      Make a jackass of you?

TOUJOURS LE VIEUX BAYOU

J'aime à le voir ainsi, calme, silencieux,
Reflétant sur son sein l'immensité des cieux.
Au milieu de ses eaux chaque étoile se place :
Je vois Orion, Vénus, comme dans une glace :
Je contemple Sirius, l'énorme Jupiter,
Le grand Saturne, et Mars sur son casque de fer.
Ils se regardent tous dans ce bayou modeste.
Je les vois de si près, que la voûte céleste
Me semble descendue de son immensité ;
Et là, tout seul, je rêve à l'immortalité ;
Et je me dis, plongé dans le doux crépuscule :
Celui qui ne croit pas… mérite la férule.

STILL THE OLD BAYOU

I love to see it thus, silent, at rest,
Reflecting heaven's expanse over its breast,
Amid its waters. There, each star in place:
Orion, Venus, mirrored... And my face
Turned toward huge Jupiter, Saturn the great,
Sirius, warrior Mars... They contemplate
Themselves in this humble bayou. I see
Them, one and all, so very close to me
That the celestial vault seems to have come
Down to earth from its vast imperium.
Here, alone, I sit with my dreams a spell,
Musing on life immortal; and I tell
Myself, shade-deep, once day has gently waned:
"Those unbelievers!... Let their likes be caned!"

TOUT PASSE

Dédié à Alcée Fortier
Pour son ancien professeur et ami.

Oui tout passe ici-bas ; on ne le voit que trop ;
Tout s'envole, tout fuit, comme un cheval au trot.
La tiare au Vatican, le chêne, le roseau,
Toute matière, hélas ! retourne à la poussière,
Du berceau dans la tombe. « Angélique prière,
« Toi seule es immortelle à genoux devant Dieu,
« Ce Dieu bon qui t'écoute en tout temps, en tout lieu. »

L'enfance balbutie ainsi que la vieillesse
Des mots divins remplis d'amour et de tendresse.
C'est toi, douce prière, émanation de ciel
Toi qui remplis nos cœurs et de myrrhe et de miel
C'est toi le talisman qui fait que l'homme adore
Et qu'il garde en son cœur la boîte de Pandore.
Heureux celui qui vient sous ton souffle enchanteur
Te dire à deux genoux : « je te donne mon cœur,
Ô prière divine, ô source de Bonheur ! »

La joue au doux duvet sous la rose splendide
S'arrondissant toujours sous les doigts de Cupide
Un jour se flétrira sous les coups du Destin…

ALL RUNS ITS COURSE

For Alcee Fortier,
old teacher and friend

Yes, my friend, here below all runs its course:
It flies, it flees, swift as a trotting horse.
Even the pope's tiara—and, perforce,
The oak, the reed... Everything falls to dust,
Cradle to tomb... "O angel prayer, you must,
Alone, be deathless, there, on bended knee,
As God gives ear in boundless clemency."

Our childhood babbles—and old age no less—
Divine words full of love and tenderness.
You, gentle prayer, of heaven sprung, rise thence
To fill our hearts with myrrh and frankincense,
You, worship's talisman... With you, man locks
Away, within his breast, Pandora's box.
Happy is he, who, charmed by your design,
Kneeling, will say: "Here, take this heart of mine,
O source of happiness, O prayer divine!"

The down-soft cheek, pink as a rose today,
Plump beneath Cupid's fingers, will give way
And wilt before the blows of Destiny.

Hélas ! la rose aussi là-bas dans le jardin,
Le jardinier aussi. Sous la faux implacable
Tout tombe ; ingrat, fidèle, innocent et coupable.

Oui, tout passe ici-bas : humilité, grandeur…
Tout croule autour de nous, mon ami, fors l'honneur.

So too the garden rose; and even he,
The gardener! All fall to the scythe, outspent—
Proud, humble, false, true, guilty, innocent...

Yes, here below all runs its course... Then wanes,
Crumbles, my friend... Honor alone remains.

Alcée Fortier: One of the earliest students of Louisiana Creole, Fortier (1856–1914) was a distinguished professor of French at Tulane University and, with Alfred Mercier, among others, a leading scholar in the culture, language, and literature of the state.

JÉSUS SUR LA CROIX

Dédié à une pieuse Mère.

Il est là suspendu sur le gibet infâme
Celui qui vient mourir pour racheter mon âme.
Sur la croix du martyr je le vois expirant…
Pour moi, pour vous, pour tous, il vient verser son sang.
Il a subi l'affront du misérable apôtre,
Le *faux*, le scélérat… qui maintenant se vautre
Dans la fange et la flamme au tréfonds de l'enfer
Avec *l'autre* damné… son ami Lucifer.

Au pied de cette croix où le Seigneur expire
L'ami verse des pleurs, et l'Apôtre soupire…
Et Marie est debout, et contemple les cieux !
Nul pleur n'obscurcit le regard de ses yeux.
Stabat en sa douleur… *Stabat* en son courage !
Cette mère chrétienne, ainsi que le roi Mage
Qui vint pour adorer Jésus en son berceau,
Adore aussi son fils qui pardonne au bourreau,
À ce bourreau qui raille et rit sur ce Calvaire
Où Jésus veut mourir pour racheter la terre.

* * *

Tu ne l'as pas compris, pauvre Pilate. Oh ! non…
Tu ne l'as pas compris… et tu fus un *poltron*.

JESUS ON THE CROSS

For a pious Mother

From the foul gibbet-cross he hangs suspended,
He, who to save my soul his days has ended.
I see him on martyrdom's cross, undone,
Gasping his last, for me, you, everyone,
Shedding his blood... He brooked the vicious shame
Of that apostle—false!—whom muck and flame
Of hell's deepest recesses now consume
With Lucifer, his friend, partner in doom.

There, at that cross's foot; there, where now dies
The Christ, the friend weeps, the Apostle sighs...
There Mary stood, her eyes turned heavenward.
Stabat, in grief, in courage, by the Lord...
Stabat, this worthy Christian mother, she,
Like a Wise King, one of the Magi three
Come to adore the cradled Jesus, her
Son, who pardons his executioner,
Who, mocking, makes great sport on Calvary,
Where Jesus wants to die to set man free.

* * *

You knew him not, O wretched Pilate. No!
You knew him not, you, lowliest of the low.

Stabat: the opening word of "Stabat mater," a medieval Catholic hymn that
expresses Mary's suffering during the crucifixion, and whose first line is
Stabat mater dolorosa ("The sorrowful mother was standing").

LE RETOUR DES OISEAUX

Dédié à « la sirène du bayou Saint-Jean. »

Ne vous envolez plus, oiseaux, vers les campagnes,
Que ce soit plaine, ou lac, ou sommets de montagnes.
C'est triste ici sans vous. Restez, restez, oiseaux,
Au bord du vieux bayou couronné de roseaux.
Pourquoi chercher au loin la grâce et l'harmonie,
Ces doux trésors du ciel, ces charmes de la vie,
Lorsque vous possédez ici... là... parmi vous
Ces sons mélodieux dont Orphée est jaloux ?
Non, non, si vous ouvrez vos ailes gracieuses,
Si vous faites vibrer vos voix délicieuses,
Que ce soit parmi vous, et les autres oiseaux
Qui reviennent au nid, à leurs petits berceaux,
Que la brise du soir balance au bord des eaux.
Chantez donc, oh ! chantez de vos voix les plus douces,
Fraîches comme les pleurs qui découlent des mousses.
Vous direz que je suis égoïste... eh bien, oui !...
Oui, Blanche, pour ta voix... demain, comme aujourd'hui,
Elle sera toujours la voix de la Sirène
Qui vint bercer Ulysse entouré de sa chaîne.

THE RETURN OF THE BIRDS

To "the Siren of Bayou Saint-Jean"

Please, birds, I pray you fly no more away,
Off to the country, mountains, lake, plains… Stay!
Stay here by this reed-garlanded bayou.
It is too sad without you here. Why do
You look for harmony and grace afar—
Life's charms and heaven's treasures—when you are,
Yourselves, the very source of melodies
That move fair Orpheus to jealousies
Galore? No, no! If you take feathered flight
On grace-blessed wings, or if your song's delight
Goes trilling roundabout, I pray you be
Surrounded by your fellows, tenderly
Returning to their cradle-nests, aloft,
Swaying in evening's breezes, calm and soft,
Over the water's edge… Sing, sing! Oh, yes,
Sing with your voices' sweetest gentleness,
Cool as the tears that from the mosses fall…
Selfish? I am! For me, that Siren call,
O Blanche, tomorrow like today! That sound
That lulled the chained Ulysses, captive bound.

STELLA MATUTINA

En ouvrant ma fenêtre aux reflets de l'aurore,
Je la vois qui scintille... elle rayonne encore ;
Mais quand l'œil flamboyant du splendide Apollon
S'ouvre, Stella pâlit... Mais à l'autre horizon,
Lorsque le dieu du jour dans les roseaux repose,
Alors Stella triomphe... elle est reine... elle pose,
Se reflète dans l'onde et règne dans les cieux.
C'est l'heure où Cupidon vient d'un air sérieux
Réveiller la jeunesse en lui bandant les yeux.
Eh ! qui n'a pas souri... voyons... même à mon âge,
En voyant le carquois de ce beau petit page ?
(Car il fut pour sa mère un page-ambassadeur
Dont la mission était... de captiver le cœur.)
Il s'en acquitte bien, pas vrai, Corinne... Jeanne ?
Dans le palais des rois, comme dans la cabane...

STELLA MATUTINA

I open wide my window on the darkling
Sky, as dawn rises, and I see her, sparkling
Still—morning star… And when Apollo's eye
Casts its rays, flaming, through the brightening sky,
Stella grows pale… But when, come eventide,
Among the reeds, down by the other side—
The near horizon—she reposes, then
Stella is queen, and, brilliant once again,
In triumph reigns: the hour when Cupid, he
Of serious mien, approaches stealthily
To waken youth and band its eyes! Look! See?
Who—even I, age-bowed!—has never smiled
Before the quiver of that darling child,
Whose mother chose him as her page, with dart
And arrow to subdue each lover's heart?
Well done!… Regal Corinne and humble Jeanne?
In hut or palace… Lovelorn, everyone!

Stella matutina: Latin for "morning star," personified here in the company of
the poet's other loves.

LA DÉFENSE DE L'ÂNE

Eh ! qui n'a pas chanté ce pauvre pâtira
Dont toujours on a ri, dont toujours on rira !
Croyez-vous qu'il n'ait pas tout autant de cervelle
Que le coursier fougueux qui bondit sous la selle ?
On ne peut, il est vrai, parmi les animaux
Le citer, sans caution, comme l'un des plus beaux,
Mais faut-il pour cela qu'il soit un misérable
Qu'on doive reléguer dans un coin de l'étable ?
Il me semble au contraire, à défaut de beauté,
Que la nature eût dû pencher de son côté,
Et balancer la chose un peu mieux envers l'âne,
Lui donner plus d'entrain et le rendre plus crâne ;
C'est tout ce qui lui manqué ; — et si vous m'en croyez,
Aimez Aliboron ; — et si vous le choyez,
Vous trouverez en lui le serviteur fidèle,
L'ami de la maison, le travailleur modèle
Dont les pas assurés, et par monts et par vaux
Vous aideront toujours à porter les fardeaux.

Au fait, pourquoi rit-on quand on parle de l'âne,
Et pourquoi sans raison lui cherche-t-on chicane ?
Ah ! si la pauvre bête oubliée en son coin
Savait bien s'exprimer tout en mangeant son foin,
Bon Dieu ! comme il rirait en considérant l'homme
En tout ce qu'il a fait depuis Ève et sa pomme.

DEFENSE OF THE ASS

Who has not sung the woes, and chortled on
And on, about the suffering, woebegone,
Poor ass? Who has not laughed and chaffed, and loudly
Mocked him! No stallion he, who courses proudly,
Wildly, beneath the saddle! And, far less
Is he an emblem fair of loveliness
Incarnate! No! But is it fitting, thus,
That we heap him with scorn opprobrious
And throw him to the stable's innermost
Recess? Rather must nature, gentle host,
Have lavished on him greater dignity,
To compensate him, ugly though he be,
With energy and stubbornness; for those
Are asses' most essential qualities...
Yes, take my word and love Aliboron;
Treat him with kindness: ever and anon.
He shall a faithful servant be, and will,
Sure-footed creature, over vale and hill
Help you, however weighty be the pack
You cast upon his broad and doughty back.

Indeed, why do we laugh when ass is mentioned?
Why must we be so crass, nasty-intentioned
In his regard? If he could speak—away
Off in his comer, champing on his hay—
How he would laugh at man, good God! and all
His evils since Eve's apple and his fall!

« Pauvre bafoué dira le juste et bon fermier,
Je t'aime et t'apprécie : tu seras le premier
À l'étable, au mangeoir, dans mon gras pâturage
Où chacun humblement saura te rendre homage ;
Car, quel est l'animal qui soit moins ignoré,
Plus doux, quoique têtu, qui fût plus honoré
Que l'âne fabuleux qui parla comme un homme,
Qu'on a connu partout, d'Athènes jusqu'à Rome ?
Il fut conférencier du temps de Barlaam
Et le seul porte-paix du fermier Abraham. »

Oui, oui, messieurs, son nom, et sa digne personne
Parmi les animaux méritent la couronne ;
Car, sans aller plus loin, je le vois en honneur
Puisqu'il porte humblement son maître, le Seigneur.
Il ne fléchira pas, sa mission est trop belle...
Il n'est plus l'âne obscur à l'allure rebelle ;
Il sait que sur son dos repose le Sauveur...
Il se sent tout couvert et de gloire et d'honneur ;
Il sait par ce seul fait vraiment digne d'envie
Qu'il ne pâtira plus... là-bas, dans l'autre vie.

Ainsi, disons que l'âne, honoré, ennobli,
N'est pas un animal qui soit digne d'oubli,
Mais admirons plutôt ce serviteur fidèle :
Quoique nul ne l'ait vu bondissant sous la selle,
Ne lui préférez pas l'imbécile chameau,
Car vous voyez que l'âne est encor bien plus beau.
Il sait se faire aimer en se faisant connaître,
Et s'il n'est un amour... il est digne de l'être.
Il a subi partout le sort du pâtira
Et de ce que j'ai dit malheur à qui rira.

Va donc, et dors en paix, emblème de patience ;
Quoique tu ne sois pas un vrai puits de science,

90

"O you, poor butt of scorn," will say the good
And worthy farmer. "You, whose hardihood
I love and prize; you who will be the beast
Most esteemed of my stable; first to feast
At the trough, feeding, and the first to stand
Grazing at will on my rich pastureland...
Who, better known than you, of fabled tongue—
Obstinate, true, but eloquent among
Romans, Greeks, and in days of Barlaam,
And who preached peace to farmer Abraham?"

Indeed, friends, worthy he to wear the crown—
With honor—of fair animal renown.
No other proof need I put forth... Look! See
Him bear his Lord in pure humility!
He will not flinch in this fine task of his.
His Savior on his back, he knows he is
Not that mere ass obscure he was before,
But transformed, decked in glory evermore.
Envied for sure is he; for he, in sum,
No woes will suffer in the life to come.

Thus be it said, the noble ass's lot
Is not to be disparaged or forgot.
Rather, let us this servant true admire,
Though never does his saddle seem afire
With speed! Finer than stupid camel, he.
And prettier too, I think you will agree!...
And if he is, indeed, no fount of love,
Once known to us he earns the fruits thereof.
Innocent beast, much has he suffered, whence
Woe unto him who laughs at my defense!

Emblem of patience, sleep in peace. Though you
Are no symbol of wisdom—all too true!—

Si dans les cieux
Auprès des dieux
On te fait place,
Tu seras là l'élu
Du bon Jésu
Et l'honneur de ta race.

When heaven's grace
Bestows your due,
Grants you a place
On high, you will abide,
By Jesus' side,
The honor of your race.

Aliboron: The name traditionally given to the ass by La Fontaine in his *Fables*. Etymologically, it is generally thought to derive from the hellebore (in Latin, *elleborum*), a medicinal plant known from ancient times and eventually associated with pretentious charlatans. Others trace it to the Arab mathematician Al-Birouni (962–1048).

Barlaam: Medieval Indian holy man and teacher, whose story parallels that of the Buddha, and who eventually was incorporated into Christian hagiography.

NOS PÈRES

J'entends leurs voix d'ici, de ma chambre, au bayou,
Au beau bayou St-Jean si tranquille et si doux…
J'écoute, et je me dis : « Où sont ces centenaires,
Ces sages d'autrefois que nous nommons nos pères ?
L'herbe ne pousse pas autour de leurs tombeaux ;
Nos genoux l'ont flétrie mieux que n'eût fait la faux.
Que sont-ils devenus ? du haut du ciel splendide
Parmi tous ces soleils où l'Éternel réside,
Qui nous dit que là-bas, au sein du firmament
Chaque étoile ne soit leur sourire d'antan
Qui descendait jadis sur nos têtes d'enfant ? »

Vous dites que la mort, cruelle, impitoyable,
A réduit au néant ce beau vieillard aimable,
Cet aïeul que l'enfant adorait à genoux ?
Non, non, il est resté sacré pour vous, pour nous.
Qu'a donc fait cette mort qu'on dit si redoutable ?
Ne la crains pas, enfant ; elle n'est effroyable
Que lorsque le coupable est tombé sous sa faux
Et que la mort lui crie : « aux flammes, il le faut. »
Mais nos pères, oh ! non. Ils sont au ciel… étoiles,
Soleils, lumière, amour, sans ombres et sans voiles.

Regardez-les, enfants, ces étoiles là-bas…
Regardez-les toujours, ne les oublions pas.
Chaque étoile est un œil, un regard de nos pères
Qui nous dit : « Aimez-vous, car vous êtes tous frères. »

OUR FATHERS

I hear their voices from my room close by
The fair Bayou Saint-Jean, whose waters lie
So tranquil, calm... I give ear, and I say:
"Where are those hundred-year-old sages, they
Of yesteryear, who are 'our fathers' called?
Their graves stand barren now, the ground stripped bald,
Where, more than bladed scythe, our bended knees
Withered the grasses that once grew? Where, these
Fine forebears? Who will tell us that each star,
Each sun, where the Eternal dwells—afar,
On high—is not, in fact, a smile they smiled
Upon the head of each yesterday's child?"

What? Do you say that death—cruel, pitiless—
Has reduced unto utter nothingness
That gentle elder, that ancestor, who
Earned a child's kneeling worship? No. For you,
For us, still is he blessed. What has death done
To make it fearsome so? No need, my son...
None but the wretch, scythed down by death, does well
To fear its cry: "Into the flames of hell!"
But not our fathers! No. In heaven, bright
They dwell: stars, suns, love, casting clear their light.

Look at them, children. See those stars on high...
Forget them not: each star, a father's eye,
A gaze of theirs, that says: "Love one another.
For you are, one and all, each one, our brother."

LE SIGNE DE LA CROIX

Il descend calme et doux près des fonts baptismaux
Sur un seul petit être, ou bien sur des jumeaux.
Ils ont la clef du ciel… Leurs mains douces et belles
Leur ouvrent les portails des voûtes éternelles.
L'eau sainte les bénit… ou jumeaux ou jumelles.
Que ce soit *elle* ou *lui*, qu'importe le minois
De ces anges humains qui sourient sous la croix !
Qu'importe qu'ils soient là, vagissant *quelquefois* ?

Plus tard, sur le beau front des mêmes petits anges
Qu'on a vus souriants, doux et purs dans leurs langes,
Le signe de la croix, ce sourire du ciel
Qui nous remplit le cœur et de « myrrhe et de miel »
Descend calme et serein. Devant l'autel, la tête
De l'ange d'autrefois en un beau jour de fête
Se penche avec amour et reçoit dans son cœur
Cette grâce du ciel, le sang du Rédempteur.

Plus tard encore, (Oh ! joie éclatante, splendide…)
Ô croix qui fais vibrer l'âme pure et candide,
Au pied du même autel. Ô croix, tu viens bénir
Deux cœurs remplis d'amour pour un doux avenir.

Ensuite… Ô sombre mort, tu viens avec ta faux
Pour nous faire pâlir au bord de nos tombeaux,
Mais là, nous sourions à ce signe suprême
Qui vient nous couronner comme d'un diadème.

THE SIGN OF THE CROSS

By the baptismal fonts serene, it taps
Gently a lone babe's head, or twins perhaps,
All who the key to heaven possess... Their hands—
Fair, soft—open the portal-vaults where stands
Eternity... Blessed by the holy water,
Be they one, be they two—twin son, twin daughter—
Despite their newborn shrieks, the cross's grace
Lights up these human angels' smiling face!

Later, over the smiling brow of those
Same angels pure, fair in their swaddling-clothes,
That heavenly smile, sign of the cross—whose balm
Of "myrrh and honey" fills our hearts—spreads, calm
And tranquil... And the angel bows its head
Altarward; angel love-engarlanded
In festive joy... And in its heart, the flood
Of heaven's grace flowing: the Redeemer's blood.

Later still... Cross! Resplendent joy! O you,
Who stir the spotless soul! Now there stand two,
At the same altar's foot... O cross, you bless
Two hearts, love-filled, with lifelong tenderness...

At length... O gloom of death, like scythe of doom
You come, make us grow pale astride the tomb.
Yet still we smile upon this priceless gem:
This sign that crowns us like a diadem.

L' ARBRE DU GRAND-PÈRE

Il est là, devant moi… j'aime à le voir ici,
Ce lilas tout en fleurs… j'aime à le voir ainsi !

Je l'ai pris tout petit au sortir de la graine ;
Adonc, il eut son gland tout comme le gros chêne.
Et depuis, ses rameaux comme des bras humains
S'allongent en souriant pour me prendre les mains.
Il m'attire sous lui, puis, là, son frais ombrage
Descend tranquille et beau. Qu'il est doux à mon âge
De m'asseoir là, tout seul, sans soupir, sans douleur ;
Ou… de voir folâtrer *ces amours de mon cœur,*
De mon vieux cœur aimant, autour de moi, grand-père.
Oh ! que j'aime à les voir, et la sœur et le frère…
Eux, se roulant sur l'herbe, et moi leur souriant.
Oui, mon bonheur est tel que je prie en riant…

C'est un vrai Briarée, ce bel arbre que j'aime,
Et que j'ai vu grandir, que j'ai planté moi-même.
Venez, venez le voir, l'arbre que j'ai planté,
Qui touche à ma fenêtre et que j'ai tant chanté ;
Et vous direz : Salut! comme moi, moi dès l'aube,
Dans un tel paradoxe que l'on est loin de Job !!

GRANDFATHER'S TREE

This lilac tree in flower... I love to see
This lilac tree, blooming in front of me!

I took it as a seedling, nurtured it,
Till, like an oak, it sprouted and grew fit
To sow its seed... Now, boughs outspread, it stands,
Smiling, like someone reaching for my hands.
It draws me to its shade, invites me there,
In its descending shadow, to come share
Its cool tranquility... How sweet, with all
My years, to sit, without a sigh, and loll
Alone... Or smile—proud grand-papá—as my
Darlings—brother and sister—charm my eye
With folderol and frolic... Such the sight,
That, calm, I mutter prayers of delight...

Mighty Briareus, this tree I love;
Tree that, myself, I planted; tree whereof
I sing... Come, see how high it grows, until
It reaches even to my window sill.
And, you will say, greeting the dawn like me:
"How far from Job, the comforts of this tree!"

Briareus: In Greek mythology, one of the hundred-handed giants, son of
Uranus and Gaea—Heaven and Earth—who used his great strength in a
variety of services to Zeus and the gods.

MON VIEUX BAYOU SAINT-JEAN

Qu'il est beau ce bayou que j'aime, que j'admire !
J'adore son méandre, et l'air qu'on y respire.
Il serpente en silence au milieu des roseaux,
À l'ombre des géants que reflètent ses eaux.
On dirait d'un boa se déroulant dans l'ombre,
Gracieux et tranquille. On ne voit rien de sombre,
Tout est riant ici… Surtout quand dans les bois
Les habitants des airs nous charment de leurs voix.
Si vous n'avez pas vu ce contour, cette grâce
Qui se répand partout sur toute sa surface,
Dirigez donc vos pas vers ses bords enchanteurs ;
Et là, des souvenirs feront rêver vos cœurs.

Vous verrez l'arbre roi qui se penche sur l'onde,
Et vous dit qu'autrefois, sous lui, tout à la ronde,
Les indiens Tchoutchoumas, assis au bord de l'eau,
Le calumet en main, humaient, d'un long tuyau,
Le parfum du tabac qui montait en spirale.
Vous y verrez Orion ; et Vénus la rivale
De Jupiter lui-même… ! Ô beau ciel étoilé,
Que la main d'Apollon n'a pas encore voilé !

Tout ce monde céleste en cette nuit profonde
Scintille… et vient perler la surface de l'onde :
Miroir digne des cieux, mon paisible bayou !
Ici point de caquet, point de cancan, point de voyou,
Mais le cœur plein d'amour, mais le cœur plein de joie

MY OLD BAYOU SAINT-JEAN

How beautiful, this bayou mine! I love
Its twists and turns, the air wafting above...
It snakes in silence through the reeds, amid
Reflected giants... Like a boa that slid,
Slithered out of the shade, and will appear
In slow, graceful uncoilings... Nothing here
Bespeaks the dour, the grim. Everything smiles,
Like chirp of woodland birds, voice that beguiles
Our ear. Ah! If the comely, shapely grace
That overspreads the waters' gentle face
Has never met your eye, pray come to these
Enchanting shores, to dream heart's memories.

Here will you see that king of trees, that leans
Over the waves, where, by its trunk, grand scenes
Of Indian braves—the Chouchoumas—were played,
As, on the ground, peace-pipe in hand, they made
The round, inhaling, through its slender stem,
Tobacco smoke, whose scent rose over them
In swirling clouds... Orion will you see
As well; and Venus, beauteous rival, she,
Of Jupiter!... a lovely sky, star-limned,
That bright Apollo's hand has not yet dimmed!

The dark-deep night of this celestial world
Sparkles over the water's surface, pearled
Mirror most heaven-worthy, calm bayou!

Nous disons l'*Angelus* en regardant la croix ;
La croix sur ce clocher qui là-bas monte et brille
Cette croix du Chrétien qui rayonne et scintille.

No chattering tongues, no crass hullabaloo
Clattering through the peace... Heart rapturous,
Eyes on the cross, we pray the *Angelus;*
The cross atop the steeple, rising high,
Cross of the Christians, glittering on the sky.

Bayou Saint-Jean: see page 12.

Chouchoumas: a warlike people of the southern Mississippi, eventually merged with the Choctaws.

L'ATTENDU

Sous les rameaux ombreux du chêne séculaire
Son regard inquiet, vers l'horizon lointain,
      Errait sur les flots bleus.
      Courage, pauvre mère
Tu reverras ton fils dans tes bras… sur ton sein.

Dieu veille sur ses jours, et l'ange tutélaire
Qui vint s'asseoir jadis au bord de son berceau,
Le tient… là… sous son aile, et l'enfant téméraire
Te reviendra bientôt ramené par le flot.

Elle attend… mais au loin, elle aperçoit l'orage
Qui soulève les mers et fait pâlir son cœur.
Tout à coup, éperdue, et malgré son courage,
Elle se précipite en proie à la terreur.

Mais le fils a grandi sous le drapeau des braves
Qui suivirent ses pas triomphants, glorieux ;
Sa volonté de fer ne connut point d'entraves ;
Il fut placé partout parmi les demi-dieux.

Redresse-toi, reviens… calme-toi, brave femme ;
Il fut vainqueur cent fois, ton fier et noble fils.
Des bouts de l'univers la Victoire l'acclame.
L'enfant est revenu le héros d'Austerlitz!!

THE AWAITED

Peering afar in hundred-year oak's shade,
Anxious, the mother pressed her gaze's quest
      Over the waves of blue.
      Poor soul, be not afraid:
Your arms will hold him, clasp him to your breast.

God guards him; and that watchful angel who
Sat by his cradle, holds him tenderly
Under her wing... That child of derring-do
Will soon return to you, over the sea.

She waits... Off in the distance, forming there,
She sees the storm splashing the waves... Heart pale
With desperate terror, but devil-may-care,
She lurches forth into the lashing gale.

But he had grown in valor, flag-protected
On triumph's glorious path... Against all odds,
His iron will a bulwark had erected,
And he stood proud among the demigods.

Come back, madame! Fear not for such a one!
Return he will! Victory showers its
Fame universal on your noble son,
Hundred-fold hero, pride of Austerlitz!!

Austerlitz: Site of the famous epic battle in which, on December 2, 1805, the troops of Napolean I crushed the forces of Russia and Austria commanded by Czar Alexander and Holy Roman Emperor Francis II. It is generally considered Napolean's greatest victory.

ELLE ET LUI

Morne ; silencieux, il se promène à l'ombre
Des rameaux ondoyants de son royal château,
Où pleure Joséphine, épouse triste et sombre,
Dont le cœur est navré comme au bord d'un tombeau.

Laisse couler tes pleurs… Le martyre en ce monde
Vient du ciel, entends-tu, du ciel bleu qui te dit :
« Tout rayonne là-haut pour la douleur profonde,
Pour toi, pauvre colombe, aux pieds de ce bandit. »

Il sait que ton amour est un amour quand même
Qui se donne à jamais. Il le sait bien, l'ingrat…
Mais il sent en son cœur, hélas ! que ceux qu'il aime
Se nomment *Masséna, Ney, Lannes et Murat.*

Il ignorait que là, celle qui le supplie
À genoux, délaissée, aux portes du trépas,
L'adorait pour son cœur et non pour son génie.

« Adieu, lui dit le Corse, ils m'attendent là-bas…
— Adieu », lui dit l'épouse, en lui tendant les bras.

SHE AND HE

Silent, somber, he paces fro and to,
There in the chateau's swaying branches' gloom,
Where Joséphine, heart-sore with bitterest rue,
Weeps like one casting tears upon a tomb.

Let flow your tears... Martyrdom here below
Shines from on high, from the blue sky above,
Saying: "All heaven's light brightens your woe,
Kneeling before that cad, O poor, dear dove."

He knows your love will neither waver nor
Grow cold. His be it ever, come what may,
The brute! Yet in his heart he loves far more
Those named *Masséna, Murat, Lannes, and Ney*...

Nor did he realize that she, who, still
At death's door, knelt before his very eyes,
Adored him for his heart, not for his skill.

"They wait for me," the Corsican replies,
"Farewell..." And, arms outstretched, "Farewell," she sighs...

Masséna, Murat, Lannes, Ney: names of several important Napoleonic generals, rivals for Empress Joséphine's attention.

MON PREMIER COQ

Je me souviens de lui, de ce coq triomphant
Qui venait se percher sur mes genoux d'enfant.
Je le vois, je l'entends quand de sa voix stridente
Il faisait vibrer l'air, — quand sa prunelle ardente
Lançait de l'escarboucle un rayon flamboyant
Que réflétaient sa tête et sa crête de sang.
Son superbe panache aussi flottait au vent,
Tel celui du grand roi qui régna sur la France
Et dont tout l'univers reconnut la vaillance.
Mon coq chargeait toujours, et souvent d'un seul coup
Terrassait l'adversaire en lui cassant le cou.
On l'appelait Bayard, l'ennemi de la broche,
Comme l'autre, il mourut « sans peur et sans reproche. »

Il eut un petit *cuic*, un *cuic* intéressant
Un soir qu'il vit le jour, petit poulet naissant,
Et moi de le gâter, tout comme un petit frère,
Je me sentais heureux de lui servir de mère.
Mais bientôt son *cuic* devint un vrai clairon
Qui retentit dans l'air, dès l'aube, à l'horizon.

Il n'était plus poulet, mon coq aux larges ailes.
Quand dans la basse cour voyant un tas de belles
Se promener au frais à l'ombre du Sachem
Haut la crête il entrait, comme à Jérusalem
Entre le Turc vainqueur, chez lui, dans son harem…
C'était bien son harem, à ce coq, magnanime,
Qui pour avoir raison n'attendait pas la rime,
Car là, sans plus tarder, préconisant l'amour,
Il captivait les cœurs comme un vrai troubadour.

MY PET COCK

I well recall that cock, who would come stand
Perched on my young lad's lap; who proudly fanned
The rustling air, with cry so sharp, so shrill,
That I can see him here and hear him still;
As when his eye—a gem of blood-bright red—
With that triumphant flourish of the head,
Reflected on his crest, tuft-garlanded…
It fluttered, wind-blown, like those fine plumes worn
By the famed king of France, to valor born.
Bold, he would charge the enemy, and broke
Many a neck with but a single stroke.
As for the spit, he had the haughtiest sneer!
Bayard we named him: like that "cavalier
Fearless, beyond reproach," who would face death
With hero's calm, breathing his final breath.

One night, when he was hatched, my newborn chick
Cackled a little *clak*, a little *clik*,
And I began to spoil him as if he—
Son? Brother?—were part of our family.
But soon his *clik* grew to dawn's trumpet-blare,
Horizon to horizon, through the air.

No longer now my little chick, friend cock,
Grown broad of wing, who, penned, took ample stock
Of belles flocking about their Sachem—he
Like knight who, in Jerusalem, made free
Among the conquering Turks, as he would seem
Master of his seraglio, his hareem…
Strutting his reason—with no thought of rhyme—
Demanding love of all the hens each time
He plied them with each amorous overture,
He won their hearts like a true troubadour.

Un jour, un de ses fils, fatigué de l'audace
De ce frère tyran, opprobre de sa race,
S'arrêta tout à coup et lui fit volte-face.
Un combat s'engagea qui fit couler le sang…
Pourquoi se battaient-ils ?… Je vous le donne en cent.
C'était tout simplement pour les grasses donzelles,
Qui riaient de les voir s'exterminer pour elles.

Bezelbuth enterra mon vieux coq un beau jour
Lui-même fatigué de voir un tel amour.

Bayard mourut enfin presque à la fleur de l'âge,
Brave jusqu'à la mort et coq de son village.

Bayard: Pierre Terrail, seigneur de Bayard (1473–1524) was a celebrated French soldier-knight, known in history and literature as the "chevalier sans peur et sans reproche."

One day, one of his sons (or brothers?) who
Was fed up with his cock-a-doodle-doo
Tyrannical, scourge of his race, fell to,
Turned a gruff back on him. Combat ensued,
Blood flowed… Why? Guess! The belles, in flattered mood,
Watch as each kills the other for their love,
Delighted to have been the cause thereof.

One day, Beelzebub, tired of such passion,
Buried my poor old cock in proper fashion.

So died Bayard, still in his prime: pet, friend,
Proud village cock, a hero to the end.

NORMAN R. SHAPIRO, honored as one of the leading contemporary translators of French, holds the B.A., M.A., and Ph.D. from Harvard University and, as Fulbright scholar, the *Diplôme de Langue et Lettres Françaises* from the Université d'Aix-Marseille. He is Professor of Romance Languages and Literatures at Wesleyan University and is currently Writing and Theater Adviser at Adams House, Harvard University. His many published volumes span the centuries, medieval to modern, and the genres: poetry, novel, and theater. Among them are *Four Farces by Georges Feydeau*; *The Comedy of Eros: Medieval French Guides to the Art of Love*; *Selected Poems from Baudelaire's 'Les Fleurs du Mal'*; *One Hundred and One Poems of Paul Verlaine* (recipient of the Modern Language Association's Scaglione Award); *Negritude: Black Poetry from Africa and the Caribbean*; and *Creole Echoes: The Francophone Poetry of Nineteenth-Century Louisiana*.

A specialist in French fable literature, Shapiro has also published *Fables from Old French: Aesop's Beasts and Bumpkins* and *The Fabulists French: Verse Fables of Nine Centuries*. His translations of La Fontaine are considered by many to be the definitive voicing into English of this famed French poet. His critically acclaimed volumes include *Fifty Fables of La Fontaine*; *Fifty More Fables of La Fontaine*; *Once Again, La Fontaine*; and *The Complete Fables of Jean de La Fontaine*, for which he was awarded the MLA's prestigious Lewis Galantiere Prize.

His monumental collection *French Women Poets of Nine Centuries: The Distaff and the Pen* won the 2009 National Translation Award from the American Literary Translators

Association, as well as two 2008 PROSE Awards from the Association of American Publishers for the Best Single-Volume Reference in the Humanities and Social Sciences and for Excellence in Reference Works.

Other titles include *La Fontaine's Bawdy: Of Libertines, Louts, and Lechers; To Speak, to Tell You? Poems by Sabine Sicaud;* and *Préversities: A Jacques Prévert Sampler.* Shapiro is a member of the Academy of American Poets, and has been named Officier de l'Ordre des Arts et des Lettres de la République Française.

M. LYNN WEISS, associate professor of English and American literature, received her doctorate from Brandeis University in 1992. Weiss is the author of *Gertrude Stein and Richard Wright: The Poetics and Politics of Modernism* (1998), has written introductions to *The Jew of Seville* and *The Fortune Teller* by Victor Séjour (2000), and wrote the introduction and edited, *Creole Echoes: The Francophone Poetry of Nineteenth Century Louisiana* (2003). She teaches African American literature and American ethnic literature. Her interests include race, ethnicity, transnationalism, and multilingualism.

TITLES FROM BLACK WIDOW PRESS

TRANSLATION SERIES

A Life of Poems, Poems of a Life
by Anna de Noailles. Translated by Norman
R. Shapiro. Introduction by Catherine Perry.

Approximate Man and Other Writings
by Tristan Tzara. Translated and edited by
Mary Ann Caws.

Art Poétique
by Guillevic. Translated by Maureen Smith.

The Big Game
by Benjamin Péret. Translated with an
introduction by Marilyn Kallet.

Capital of Pain
by Paul Eluard. Translated by Mary Ann Caws,
Patricia Terry, and Nancy Kline.

Chanson Dada: Selected Poems
by Tristan Tzara. Translated with an
introduction and essay by Lee Harwood.

Essential Poems and Writings of Joyce Mansour:
A Bilingual Anthology
Translated with an introduction by
Serge Gavronsky.

Essential Poems and Prose of Jules Laforgue
Translated and edited by Patricia Terry.

Essential Poems and Writings of Robert Desnos:
A Bilingual Anthology
Edited with an introduction and essay by
Mary Ann Caws.

EyeSeas (Les Ziaux) by Raymond Queneau.
Translated with an introduction by Daniela
Hurezanu and Stephen Kessler.

Furor and Mystery & Other Writings
by René Char. Edited and translated by
Mary Ann Caws and Nancy Kline.

The Inventor of Love & Other Writings
by Gherasim Luca. Translated by Julian & Laura
Semilian. Introduction by Andrei Codrescu.
Essay by Petre Răileanu.

La Fontaine's Bawdy
by Jean de La Fontaine. Translated with an
introduction by Norman R. Shapiro.

Last Love Poems of Paul Eluard
Translated with an introduction by
Marilyn Kallet.

Love, Poetry (L'amour la poésie) by Paul Eluard.
Translated with an essay by Stuart Kendall.

Poems of André Breton: A Bilingual Anthology
Translated with essays by Jean-Pierre Cauvin
and Mary Ann Caws.

Poems of A.O. Barnabooth by Valéry Larbaud.
Translated by Ron Padgett and Bill Zavatsky.

Poems of Consummation by Vicente Aleixandre.
Translated by Stephen Kessler

Préversities: A Jacques Prévert Sampler
Translated and edited by Norman R. Shapiro.

The Sea and Other Poems
by Guillevic. Translated by Patricia Terry.
Introduction by Monique Chefdor.

To Speak, to Tell You? Poems by Sabine Sicaud.
Translated by Norman R. Shapiro. Introduction
and notes by Odile Ayral-Clause.

forthcoming translations

Guarding the Air:
Selected Poems of Gunnar Harding
Translated and edited by Roger Greenwald.

Pierre Reverdy: Poems Early to Late
Translated by Mary Ann Caws and
Patricia Terry.

Jules Supervielle: Selected Poems
Translated by Nancy Kline and Patricia Terry.

Boris Vian Invents Boris Vian:
A Boris Vian Reader
Edited and translated by Julia Older.

MODERN POETRY SERIES

ABC of Translation by Willis Barnstone

An Alchemist with One Eye on Fire
by Clayton Eshleman

Anticline by Clayton Eshleman

Archaic Design by Clayton Eshleman

Backscatter: New and Selected Poems
by John Olson

The Caveat Onus by Dave Brinks

City Without People: The Katrina Poems
by Niyi Osundare

Concealments and Caprichos
by Jerome Rothenberg

Crusader-Woman by Ruxandra Cesereanu.
Translated by Adam J. Sorkin. Introduction by
Andrei Codrescu.

Curdled Skulls: Poems of Bernard Bador
Translated by the author with
Clayton Eshleman.

Endure: Poems by Bei Dao. Translated by
Clayton Eshleman and Lucas Klein.

Exile is My Trade: A Habib Tengour Reader
Translated by Pierre Joris.

Fire Exit by Robert Kelly

Forgiven Submarine by Ruxandra Cesereanu and
Andrei Codrescu

from stone this running by Heller Levinson

The Grindstone of Rapport:
A Clayton Eshleman Reader

Larynx Galaxy by John Olson

The Love That Moves Me
by Marilyn Kallet

Memory Wing by Bill Lavender

Packing Light: New and Selected Poems
by Marilyn Kallet

The Present Tense of the World:
Poems 2000–2009 by Amina Saïd. Translated
with an introduction by Marilyn Hacker.

The Price of Experience by Clayton Eshleman

The Secret Brain: Selected Poems 1995–2012
by Dave Brinks

Signal from Draco: New and Selected Poems
by Mebane Robertson

forthcoming modern poetry titles

An American Unconscious by Mebane Robertson

Eye of Witness: A Jerome Rothenberg Reader
Edited with commentaries by Heriberto Yepez
& Jerome Rothenberg

Memory by Bernadette Mayer

LITERARY THEORY /
BIOGRAPHY SERIES

Revolution of the Mind: The Life of André Breton
by Mark Polizzotti

Clayton Eshleman: The Whole Art
Edited by Stuart Kendall. (forthcoming)

LOUISIANA HERITAGE SERIES
Second Line Press imprint

Jules Choppin: New Orleans Poems in
Creole and French
Translated by Norman R. Shapiro.
Introduction by M. Lynn Weiss.

Dinner at Antoine's (forthcoming)
by Francis Parkinson Keyes

WWW.BLACKWIDOWPRESS.COM